The
Promise
of
Hope

A Tribute to
Dom Hélder

The
Promise
of
Hope

Kamal Hossain
José Míguez Bonino
Tarek Mitri
Mercy A. Oduyoye
Julio de Santa Ana
Daniel S. Schipani
Bas Wielenga

Daniel S. Schipani and
Anton Wessels, editors

vrije Universiteit   *amsterdam*

Institute of Mennonite Studies

Published by Institute of Mennonite Studies, 3003 Benham Avenue, Elkhart IN 47517-1999, in collaboration with the Dom Hélder Câmara Stichting, The Free University, Amsterdam.

©2002 by Institute of Mennonite Studies

Printed in the United States of America by Evangel Press, Nappanee, Indiana

ISBN 0-936273-32-1

Library of Congress Cataloging-in-Publication Data

The promise of hope : a tribute to Dom Hélder / [contributors], Kamal Hossain … [et al.] ; Daniel S. Schipani and Anton Wessels, editors.
    p. cm.
Includes bibliographical references.
    ISBN 0-936273-32-1
    1. Câmara, Hélder, 1909– 2. Catholic Church—Bishops—Biography.
3. Bishops—Brazil—Biography. I. Câmara, Hélder, 1909– II. Hosena, Kamala.
III. Schipani, Daniel S., 1943– IV. Wessels, Antonie.
BX4705.C2625 P76 2002
282'.092—dc21
                        2002001175

Cover design by Mary E. Klassen

Cover photos and photo on p. 120 of Dom Hélder Câmara courtesy of KNA-Bild (Frankfurt)

Photos on pp. x, 140, and 141 from Vrije Universiteit archives

"Providence has taken me by the hand" courtesy of Dom Hélder Câmara estate

Let every word
be the fruit
of action and reflection.
Reflection alone
without action…
is mere theory,
adding its weight
when we are
overloaded
with it already
and it has led
the young to despair.
Action alone
without reflection
is being busy
pointlessly.
Honour the Word eternal
and speak
to make
a new world possible.

Dom Hélder Câmara
The Desert Is Fertile

Contents

Acknowledgements

The project leading to this book was initially approved by the Board of the Dom Hélder Câmara Chair at the Free University in Amsterdam, the Netherlands. It was also endorsed by the Institute of Mennonite Studies (IMS) of Associated Mennonite Biblical Seminary in the United States, and especially supported by the IMS director, Professor Mary Schertz.

Heartfelt thanks go to our colleagues, the other writers scattered in five continents, who invested time and energy to contribute their essays in the midst of their manifold commitments and responsibilities.

Students Carole Boshart and Todd Lehman were very helpful in the initial phase of the project. And Barbara Nelson Gingerich, managing editor at IMS, competently prepared the manuscript for publication, in addition to providing generous overall editorial assistance.

The publication of the book was made possible by a grant from the Vereniging voor Christelijk Wetenschappelijk Onderwijs van de Vrije Universiteit and the Radboudstichting Wetenschappelijk Onderwijsfonds, for which we are most grateful.

THE EDITORS

Dom Hélder Câmara receives the honorary doctorate in social sciences from the Free University, October 20, 1975.

Preface

Dom Hélder Câmara died on August 27, 1999, at the age of ninety. He passed away in his sleep. But the bishop's existence had always been one of continuous wakefulness as long it was day.

In 1964, he became archbishop of Olinda and Recife (he had been assistant bishop since 1952) in poor North-East Brazil. Soon he was called the "red" bishop, not because of the color of his hair (at the time), but because of his attention to the impoverished masses and the dispossessed in his region. He saw what was happening around him as the consequence of unjust international economic relationships. He learned what happens when international markets rather than local needs decide what farmers grow: Many lost their land and ended up in shantytowns (*favelas*), and many "disappeared." The over-development of the first world led to the underdevelopment of the third world.

> *When two-thirds of humanity in the world*
> *is in a state of underdevelopment,*
> *how can large amounts of money be spent*
> *in building temples of stone,*
> *and Christ's living presence*
> *in the person of the poor be forgotten?*
> *Christ is surely there,*
> *immersed in misery and hunger,*
> *living in dilapidated huts*
> *without health or job,*
> *without prospects for a future.*

Dom Hélder Câmara was the first to bring into the open the Brazilian military dictatorship's torture of its opponents (1964–1984). He wanted to initiate a "revolution in the name of peace"—the title of one of his books—a liberation through the exertion of moral pressure. Bishops and theologians of his kind were accused of meddling in politics and of defending violence in theory and in practice. Dom Hélder Câmara repeatedly responded that the social order of Latin America was itself a form of violence. His performance was characterized well by his biographer José de Broucker as *The Violence of a Peacemaker*. In this respect, he followed in the footsteps of Mahatma Gandhi and Martin Luther King, Jr.

He had another kind of church and way of being a Christian in mind than the one represented by a majority of the hierarchy of the established local Roman Catholic Church. He wanted to be a real *pontifex*, a bridge-builder. He came into conflict with the Vatican, although when Pope Paul VI was still bishop (Montini) of Milan, he was Dom Hélder's friend. But he felt uncomfortable with Dom Hélder's views. The Vatican tried to silence Dom Hélder Câmara. He became in practice an interpreter of what was to be called liberation theology. He experienced the danger of advocating an "option for the poor." Several attempts were made on his life, although he survived them, unlike Archbishop Oscar Romero of San Salvador (d. March 24, 1980). His close associate was tortured and murdered.

Did his struggle make sense? Did it produce much? Liberation theology seems in the meantime to have gone out of fashion. Several liberation theologians were killed or silenced. And since the fall of the Berlin wall, a triumphalistic capitalistic mood rules worldwide.

Dom Hélder Câmara's performance was sometimes compared with that of Don Quixote, who jousted with windmills. "I do love Don Quixote very much," Dom Helder said. "He was more a realist than one thinks." In his foolishness, this knight will continue to speak long after he has died. Dom Hélder's motto as a bishop was *"in manus tuas"*: "Into your hands I commend my spirit" (Luke 23:46), the words of the psalm (31:5) with which Jesus ended his (failed?) mission.

One of his books, *Hoping against All Hope*, includes this prayer for the rich:

> *Lord, you know well*
> *that today there are not only*
> *rich and poor individuals.*
> *There are rich, even excessively rich, countries*
> *and there are poor countries.*
> *You know, too, that the difference*
> *is becoming ever greater rather than less.*
> *Help men and women of good will—*
> *from every land and color and language and religion—*
> *to bring liberating moral pressure to bear*
> *on authorities*
> *and awaken their consciences*
> *so that they will help the human race*
> *to be freed from the shame of the subhuman beings*
> *whom wretchedness produces,*
> *and from the shame of the superhuman*
> *who are begotten of excessive prosperity and luxury.*

Help those who have the happiness
of being born in rich countries:
help them to see
that the privileges they enjoy
have been bought by injustice
to the poor countries.
Without realizing it,
they often become accomplices
of this injustice.[1]

Four times he was nominated for the Nobel Peace Prize, but it is widely assumed that forces opposed to him prevented his receiving this honor. In 1970, he was granted the Martin Luther King Jr. Award.

In 1975, the Free University in Amsterdam granted him an honorary degree. The motivation given was: Throughout his life he strove to eradicate the poverty of the people of Brazil. He worked for the social and political conscientization of his people. He made a positive contribution to the preservation of the Indian tribes threatened with extermination.

Teaching and education he saw as the levers to liberate the people from poverty and illiteracy. Therefore his activity was directed towards the child, the youth, and the family. He published many pedagogical books.

He resisted both the leadership of his church and the leadership of his country when he claimed that the interests of large groups of people were insufficiently cared for. The fact that his freedom was threatened and curtailed did not hinder him from continuing the struggle. He saw this struggle as his calling for life.

When the Free University in Amsterdam gave Dom Hélder Câmara an honorary degree in social sciences on October 20, 1975, Prof. Dr. J. W. van Hulst listed these reasons for the award: "During your whole life you were engaged in fighting against the poverty of the Brazilian people and the poverty of the entire world. You have contributed for your part in the efforts made to save Indian tribes threatened by extermination.... In this world, you have been a voice of those who are without voice, without house, without food, without clothes, without power, without work, without a future, without rights, without hope. Therefore your motto has been:

To give all you have
give all you are

---

[1] Hélder Câmara, *Hoping against All Hope,* trans. Matthew J. O'Connell (Maryknoll: Orbis Bks., 1984), 81.

giving oneself always
without ceasing to give.[2]

In his response, Dom Hélder Câmara said, among other things, that he was moved that a *Protestant* university gave him this title and that it was from a *free* university.

You encourage me to work together
to assure that liberty is not an empty word,
that liberty is not the monopoly of some.
You encourage me to work together
with all people of good will,
for liberty will really be for all,
for all people of all races,
and all religions.[3]

During a private visit at the university in November 1979 he made a "brotherly appeal to the Free University," in which he spoke about a chair of education for justice, to give attention to the unfairness of consumer society, which increasingly merits the label "society of wastefulness." The countries that produce raw materials have already been subjected to internal colonialism, practiced by the rich of underdeveloped countries who keep their riches by crushing their fellow-citizens. Then the multinationals arrive (allied to the rich groups practicing internal colonialism), promising advanced technology, more jobs, more capital, more development. What they really accomplish is the waste of still larger quantities of raw materials, the vertiginous increase of foreign debt and of unemployment, and a state of increasing tension with squatters displaced by real-estate speculation.

When I think of a chair of education for liberation,
it is in order to keep the universities from being surpassed
by the not infrequently illiterate people of the poor countries,
and by the youth of the rich countries
who, very often, faced with the impossibility
of adequately studying the great human problems in the universities,
take up self-study through matriculation in the University of Life.

The people of the poor countries are constantly learning,
the hard way,
that hate does not build anything,
that violence attracts violence,
that the appeal to arms is suicide,
since arms are manufactured by the oppressors....

---

[2] Vrije Universiteit Amsterdam, *Jaarboek 1975-1976*, 86–7.

[3] Ibid., 88.

The youth of the rich countries are discovering
with increasing clarity
various valid methods of moral liberating pressure,
in the purest spirit of active nonviolence....

The saying is, "If you want peace, prepare war."
The correct slogan would be,
"If you want peace, prepare peace."

Free University of Amsterdam, I salute you,
wishing that you may achieve freedom
and hoping that you may join forces
with your sister universities—from the north, south, west, east—
in order to help create a world in which freedom,
far from being an empty word,
may be enjoyed as one of the most precious gifts of God.

Dom Hélder spoke at the centennial anniversary of the Free University in 1980 and called for the establishment of a chair for justice, liberation, and peace. As his motivation, he mentioned that two-thirds of humankind still lives in inhuman circumstances. That is a situation of great injustice. In a country such as Brazil a kind of slavery and colonialism (now internal) still exists.[4] In the past, Catholic bishops had strong links with the rich and the government, and not with the best intentions. That seemed to be a moral thing, but today it is impossible to continue to support the social order because it is in reality a social disorder. It is our right and duty to conduct a policy of concern for the great human problems and human rights. A chair for justice is important, to open the eyes of people to injustice. Such a chair can help rich countries come to the insight that justice is the condition for peace. About the theme of liberation, he said that more and more poor countries, mainly in Latin America, are gaining the insight that seeking to reach liberation through violence is an illusion. The solution he also saw as a posture of active nonviolence.[5]

At its May 19, 1982, meeting, the college of deans of the Free University decided to establish a Dom Hélder Câmara committee, with this important task: to arrange an annual Câmara lecture (José Míguez Bonino was immediately mentioned as a possible lecturer), and to investigate the desirability and possibility of eventually establishing a Câmara chair for justice and liberation at the Free University, in cooperation with other Dutch universities.

---

[4] Recorded in *Ad Valvas* [Free University weekly newspaper], 19 June 1981.
[5] Ibid.

The Free University took up the gauntlet and established, in cooperation with the Catholic University of Nijmegen, a chair now connected with his name, "The Dom Hélder Câmara Chair." Since the 1980s, people have been nominated for the chair in the spirit of the ideals of Dom Hélder Câmara, coming from Latin America (Julio de Santa Ana and Daniel Schipani), but also from other parts of the world (Mercy Oduyoye from Africa, and Bas Wielenga from India). Recent holders of the chair include Tarek Mitri (from Lebanon), and Kamal Hossain (from Bangladesh).

Dom Hélder Câmara's warning has not lost any relevance:

University, pay attention!
Don't allow your voice to be silenced by curricula and syllabi,
which directly or indirectly are controlled by small groups,
egoistic and insatiable,
who lack the courage to face the big problems of our day.
If you are not meeting young people without fear,
open to truth, to hope, to love,
the young will replace you with the University of Life."

ANTON WESSELS

Anton Wessels is professor of missiology and history of religions (with specialty in Islam) in the Free University of Amsterdam. He has lectured widely, and is a member of the board of the Near East School of Theology, where he has also taught. He is the author of several books, including *Images of Jesus, Understanding the Qur'an, Europe: Was It Ever Really Christian?*, and *Islam Story Wise.*

When I was a youngster
I wanted to go out running
among the mountain peaks.
And when, between two summits
a gap appeared,
why not leap across the chasm?
Led by the angel's hand,
all my life long
this is what happened; this exactly.

Dom Hélder Câmara
The Violence of a Peacemaker

Throughout the course of my life,
I've come to see what a bad sign it is to be highly praised
or to receive a lot of applause.
I realize how right our Lord was
to give us that golden word:
"Let your light shine before others
so that they give glory to your Father in heaven."
God wants our works to be visible,
wants the good that we try to do to be known.
But those good works are to be done with humility,
an inner humility that is absolutely genuine....
The ideal is that the person who sees us
shouldn't even notice how wonderful and great we are.
They should find us so transparent
that instead of noticing us
they should discover the living presence of Jesus Christ.

Dom Hélder Câmara
"A Most Transparent Life"

Introduction
Honoring a Godbearing life

DANIEL S. SCHIPANI

Dom Hélder[1] used to say that if we get much praise, it is a sign that we are opaque, visible instead of transparent, as he explains in the quote on the page opposite. However, in this humble tribute we give testimony to having indeed seen him as "wonderful and great," a genuine Godbearing life. For his life became a sacrament—that is, a sign, symbol, and agent—of divine love in the world and for the sake of the world. Together with his people, he was a truthful sign, prophetically pointing in the direction of justice, peace, and the good life for humankind and the whole creation; he was also a faithful symbol representing the very hope he announced; and he was a fruitful partner of the creative, liberating, and empowering Spirit in the midst of history.

From the beginning, the forces shaping Dom Hélder's life were his robust spirituality, that is, a deep personal relationship with God; his

---

Daniel Schipani was born and raised in Argentina. He holds doctorates in psychology (Argentina Catholic University) and in practical theology (Princeton Theological Seminary). For several years he was involved in theological education in South America and the Caribbean; currently he teaches at Associated Mennonite Biblical Seminary, in the United States, and lectures as a visiting professor in several universities and theological schools in North and Latin America and Europe. Schipani has written and edited numerous books, primarily in the areas of human development, education, and pastoral theology.

[1] His full name was Hélder Pessoa Câmara. Dom Hélder's reference to how he was given his name is particularly interesting: "At the time of my birth, my father had no use for religious practices and so, instead of consulting a calendar of the saints for a name to give me, he consulted a dictionary. There he found a word that attracted him: 'HELDER, a fortified town in the northern part of the Netherlands.' And he decided to give that name to his son! In later years, some Dutch professors at a seminary I attended explained to me that in Holland, when the sky is clear, people exclaim, 'Oh, a lovely *helder* sky! Without a cloud!' I like that. It seems to mean 'without complications.'" In José de Broucker, *Dom Hélder Câmara: The Violence of a Peacemaker*, trans. Herma Briffault (Maryknoll: Orbis Bks., 1970), 137.

committed participation in the ministry of the church; and his experiences with oppression and poverty in one of the most underdeveloped regions of his native country. In due time, he became one of the Catholic church's most inspired and charismatic leaders of the twentieth century. His manifold accomplishments were simply extraordinary and they often took place in the midst of most difficult circumstances and severe opposition. It can be said that many of the social and theological concerns that revolutionized the church during the second half of the last century—the "preferential option for the poor," active nonviolence, base Christian communities, and liberation theology—could flourish in large measure because of Dom Hélder's life, work, and witness.

A physically small and slender man, standing only about five feet tall, Câmara would become a powerful public figure. Although his assigned pastoral work was meant to focus on parched and impoverished North-East Brazil, eventually his influence was felt throughout Latin American and around the world as well. And such an impact is especially remarkable in light of Câmara's proverbial simplicity, honesty, and humility.

Dom Hélder's Godbearing life consistently integrated a deep inner journey of prayer and meditation with an outward ministry of justice and peacemaking, with service to the poor, the oppressed, and the marginalized. In other words, he blended a profound spirituality with a daily practical struggle of resistance and hope. Further, he practiced what he preached. Therefore, at the end of his life journey, Dom Hélder must have received the reassuring words of his Lord: "Well done, good and trustworthy servant; you have been trustworthy in a few things, I will put you in charge of many things; enter into the joy of your master" (Matt. 25:21).

The Promise of Hope is a tribute to Dom Hélder written by scholars who have participated in the Dom Hélder Câmara Chair, at the Free University in Amsterdam, the Netherlands. This Festschrift is thus a glimpse of the international, ecumenical, and multidisciplinary import of Dom Hélder's contribution and the nature of the chair established in his honor as well. Below are the highlights of the body of this book.

In the first chapter—"Priest and prophet"—Julio de Santa Ana discusses five phases that characterized Dom Hélder's life. First, in his person priestly calling and prophetic ministry belonged together. Second, he had a strong sense of being Brazilian; he knew that his destiny was to serve the whole country. Third, being a man of great vision and initiative and a talented organizer, Dom Hélder saw the need to create a national conference of bishops in Brazil, and he was also instrumental in the formation of the Latin American Episcopal Council. Fourth, he played a leading role in drafting and disseminating the pro-liberation and justice document, "Declaration on the Situation of the Third World" (better known as the "Third World Bishops Manifesto"). Finally, he engaged in the practice of a "hidden discipleship" centering on humility and the experiences of small faith-based groups and "Abrahamic communities." Santa Ana then proceeds to reflect on the public dimension of Dom Hélder's life during turbulent years for Brazil and Latin America. He lived out his faith and his call with a prophetic voice and commitment to justice by serving the poor and confronting oppression nonviolently. Last but not least, Santa Ana highlights the rich ecumenical character of Dom Hélder's enduring legacy.

Chapter two is the contribution of Kamal Hossain, "Dom Hélder Câmara's concern for the poor: Toward a humane world order with sustainable development and human rights." It starts with the notion that the basic goal of sustainable human development is to enable all people to live in freedom and dignity. The author then presents a comprehensive discussion of the emergence and the itinerary of the concept, and the value of sustainable development, including the ongoing quest for a normative order which addresses effectively the vital concerns of the global economy and the environment. Hossain indicates that the growing body of literature underlines the multidimensional character of sustainable development and the progress of international law on this matter must begin with a proper elucidation of the concept itself. He also documents the need for a new framework in which to promote global development and protect the global environment as an overriding global objective to be secured by the universal acceptance of new principles and rules. He recognizes inherent tensions between the competing goals of environmental protection and economic develop-ment, between the goals of developed and developing states, and within an international community made up of disparate groups of states; and he makes the case for sustainable development that is "human-focused" or "people centered." Hossain thus underscores the growing awareness around the world of the integral link between sustainable development, human rights, and people's democratic participation.

In chapter three—"Reflections on eco-justice"—Bas Wielenga addresses the seemingly antagonistic, complex relationship between ecological movements and resistance to oppression and injustice. He adopts the term *eco-justice* as a means to connect both concerns, and he suggests that such a concept may be used in the wider sense of doing justice to the relationship among humans as well as between humans and non-human nature. Wielenga considers *eco-justice* particularly appropriate and useful in light of the covenant-centered biblical view of reality. He thus presents biblical and political reflections meant to highlight the inner connection between the "integrity of creation" and the struggle for social justice. Taking justice in the sharing of resources for the sake of increasing the quality of life as our aim, we find that the basic problem is not population growth or scarcity as such. The fundamental problem is the way a minority of rich countries, and the dominant classes in all countries, have appropriated and accumulated the earth's God-given resources, and used violence to deny others access to those resources. Wielenga also suggests some ways to convert the present global system to a viable "people's economy of life": drawing strength from local roots, resisting destructive global institutions and policies, forming covenant alliances against bio-piracy, defending democratic spaces, and working faithfully in the church.

Chapter four consists of Tarek Mitri's essay—"A global confrontation or local conflicts?"—which focuses on the challenges posed by the relationship between Christianity and Islam. He reminds us that both carry deep historical memories and appeal in different ways to universal loyalties. Mitri contends that, when assessing the role of religion in national or international politics, it is essential to distinguish between political movements that may be genuinely inspired by religion and those that use religion as a convenient legitimation for political agendas based on nonreligious interests. He proposes that a vital step toward resolving Christian-Muslim tensions lies in de-globalizing them. For attention to the context-specific causes of conflicts helps identify alternatives to be found, first and foremost, in addressing those local realities. Therefore, Mitri states, leaders of both communities must refuse to be drawn into the conflicts of others on the basis of uncritical responses to calls for solidarity among adherents to one faith. In applying common principles of peace, justice, and reconciliation, those party to local and regional conflicts will be helped to release Islam and Christianity from the burden of sectional interests and self-serving interpretations of beliefs and convictions. Christian and Islamic beliefs and convictions can then become foundational for critical engagement with human weakness, and with defective social and economic orders in a common search for human well-being, social justice, and peace.

Mercy Amba Oduyoye's contribution is the content of chapter five, "Peace and justice: A theological hermeneutic through one African woman's eyes." Her essay highlights the pertinence and creativity of African Women in Theology (AWIT) whose theological task is done by way of a hermeneutic of peace with justice. Women's experiences are interpreted in light of Scripture and in terms of what brings authentic shalom comprehensively understood. Oduyoye reports on some of the experiences, both historical and contemporary, that have led AWIT to that theological locus. She refers to ways African women have acted and can act for peace with justice and humanization for all in the midst of socio-religious and cultural situations that shape their lives. Thus, the exclusion of women from the arenas of political and religious power is a key theological issue. She also underscores the need to challenge the church to confront sexism, and to encourage church women to organize themselves and get involved in shaping the church's agenda. Oduyoye further considers the central place of the hope for transformation, the resulting theological emphases on empowerment, participation, and partnership, and the pivotal role of a hermeneutic of worthiness in the theological task. This is a "theology en route" which necessitates participation in solidarity within caring and supportive communities, not only for survival and resistance but for engaging in transforming action as well.

Chapter six—"Love and social transformation: A reflection on base ecclesial communities in Latin America"—presents a socio-theological reflection by José Míguez Bonino on the significance of those grassroots communities (BECs) in the quest for a new society. They are viewed as unique embodiments of what Dom Hélder Câmara called "Abrahamic communities." Míguez Bonino discusses the transforming power of the experience of mutual love and solidarity in their midst. He suggests that the BECs are the best instrument to bring together the spiritual, social, formative dimensions, and the transforming dynamics which can nurture the people in their long journey toward full humanization. He focuses on the centrality of the love motif in Latin America liberation theology and how the good news of God's unconditional acceptance is historically mediated to the "non-person" (that is, marginalized, disenfranchised people). The BECs thus become seedbeds of a humanistic democratic socialism or a social participatory democracy. They are thus profoundly political manifestations of solidarity in Christian love which seek expression in a secular political order congruent with the personalization-in-community they experience at the religious level. And the key feature of solidarity must be understood in christological as well as eschatological perspectives.

Chapter seven is the final essay in the collection, titled "Dismantling racism nonviolently: A case study in practical theology." It includes my interpretive report on an ongoing project aimed at transformation toward racial justice and reconciliation within the Mennonite Church in the United States, and it is based on qualitative empirical research. The study sought to identify, first, the fruits of the labor of the antiracism program in place and, second, the impact of the project on the understandings and normative convictions concerning peace and justice. In the first part of the essay, transformative practices are highlighted having to do with issues of leadership, education, and practical ecclesiology. In the second part, there is an illustrative list of empirically documented outcomes in the manner of significant learnings identified and recognized as such by the people involved. In the third part I underscore key theological issues and concerns that stem from the antiracism project; they point to the need to reconsider afresh peace theology as a central set of normative convictions, values, and practices. Finally, I indicate several implications that the study suggests for practical theology and for theological education as well.

The appendix is the translated speech of Dom Hélder Câmara on the occasion of his installation as archbishop of Olinda and Recife, on April 12, 1964. It has a fitting title, "Providence has taken me by the hand," and provides for us a clear window to Dom Hélder's sense of identity and vocation.

The primary purpose of writing this book has been to honor the Godbearing life of Dom Hélder Câmara. Nevertheless, that purpose is inseparable from another, directly related goal—to invite many others to join us as partners in reflection, dialogue, and action. We thus encourage readers to ponder carefully Dom Hélder's vision and legacy in light of the realities of today's world and our human longing to realize the promise of hope for a better tomorrow.

> *Hope without risk*
> *is not hope,*
> *which is believing*
> *in risky loving,*
> *trusting others*
> *in the dark,*
> *the blind leap,*
> *letting God take over....*
>
> *If only we,*
> *as brothers and sisters*
> *in greatness and misery,*
> *could find again*
> *a spark of hope.*[2]

---

[2] Hélder Câmara, *Hoping against All Hope*, trans. Matthew J. O'Connell (Maryknoll: Orbis Bks., 1984), 4–5.

The urgent problem we face is this:
How are we to eliminate,
peacefully but courageously,
the great scandal of our times:
that more than two-thirds of the human race
is living in subhuman conditions
of wretchedness and hunger.

Dom Hélder Câmara
Hoping against All Hope

Let no one be deceived as to the nature of Christ....
There is no doubt that He came to bring peace to humanity,
but not the peace of stagnant swamps,
not the peace based on injustice,
not the peace that is the opposite of humanization.
In such cases, Christ himself proclaimed
that He had come to bring strife and a sword.

Dom Hélder Câmara
Revolution through Peace

1 | *Priest and prophet*

JULIO DE SANTA ANA

L ife was hard in North-East Brazil at the beginning of the twentieth century. There was no running water, no sewer system, and no electricity. Despite all the want and hardship they had to endure, the inhabitants of the region found ways of coping, and Hélder Câmara's family was no exception. They were middle-class people. His father was a mason and a spiritualist, a civil servant and son of a newspaper publisher in Fortaleza, Ceará. Religious in his own way, he did not oppose the dominant Catholic church but was simply indifferent to it. Hélder Câmara's mother was a pious woman without being excessively devout. She had thirteen children, some of whom died in the epidemics which regularly ravaged the population. The boy who was to become a bishop began to be aware of his calling to the priesthood when he was quite young. By the age of fourteen, he had entered the seminary.

At that time, Brazil was undergoing a process of rapid change. The "Aurea" law had been passed only a few years before, putting an end to slavery, at least officially. The promulgation of this law marked the end of the empire. The first republic faced many challenges: How was it to maintain national unity among a diverse population living in such different regions? How could it prevent the existing diversity from increasing still further? The permanent dichotomy in Brazilian life has often been commented on. Ever since the land became a Portuguese colony, tension existed in the seignorial structure, symbolized by the great mansion on the *fazenda*. The subject slave population, most of African origin, lived crowded together in the *sem sala*, that vast space where they dreamed of freedom and planned ways to escape their

Julio de Santa Ana was born in Uruguay. He studied theology in Buenos Aires, and in Strasbourg, where he obtained a doctorate in religious studies. He was general secretary of Church and Society in the Latin American movement (ISAL). He worked for the World Council of Churches as director of the Commission for Church Participation in Development (CCPD). Later Santa Ana became professor of social sciences and religion at the Methodist University in São Paulo, Brazil, where he also was co-director of the Ecumenical Center for Evangelization and Popular Education Services (CESEP). He returned to Geneva in 1994 and is now a professor at the Ecumenical Institute in Bossey. He is the author of several books and numerous articles.

master's yoke. There they also tried to reestablish their links with the ancestral spirits left behind in the lands from which they had been violently abducted by the slave traders.

When the first republic was established, many African-Brazilians migrated to the southern states, chiefly to Rio de Janeiro, the country's capital. The extraordinary development of São Paulo began. This was the time of the "coffee and cream" republic; São Paulo produced the coffee, and the rest came from Minas Gerais, a cattle-ranching state. The coalition between the two extended to the national government, situated in the capital. The freed slaves contributed decisively to the economic power the states of the south acquired in the national economy, a power that also extended to the political field. The northeast region of Brazil contributed intellectuals who helped hold together the difficult process of nation building.

Masters and slaves, feudal structures and subject populations were not the only contrasts. The wealthy south contrasted starkly with the impoverished northeast. The modernization that has taken place in the southern states has not happened in those of the northeast, where traditional, archaic social and labor relations persist. The waves of migrants arriving from Europe during the early decades of the last century went mainly to the south, which was making the first timid moves towards industrialization. Their coming helped increase the social difference between the developing regions and those that continued to apply social and economic practices handed down from the colonial era and the empire.

The people of the northeast experience the meaning of under-development in their everyday lives; they know what it is to live with want, suffering, and few opportunities in life. This deprivation makes many men and women decide to leave their native land for the south. At present, São Paulo is the city in Brazil with the biggest population from the northeast. Nostalgia for their home stays with people born in Bahia, Pernambuco, Ceará, and Sergipe. Whatever the advantages they find in the south, in their hearts they remain northeasterners all their lives. Their social consciousness is strongly marked by the fact they have had no choice but to migrate in their struggle for survival.

Brazilian society has evolved, but some institutions have stood firm through all the transformations, and helped maintain a degree of stability amid the rapid changes taking place. One of these institutions is the family, the unit in which its members are socialized, which in many cases is matriarchal. Another is the religious communities, chiefly those linked to the Roman Catholic Church. While evangelical groups, especially Pentecostals, have experienced astonishing increases in the last decades of the past century, it is the Catholic communities that help make more bearable the uprooting experienced by migrants.

The evolution of Brazilian Catholicism cannot be separated from that of the Brazilian people. It is a Catholicism *sui generis,* aware that it has to be close to the people it seeks to serve; a Catholicism that responds flexibly to the tension between the expectations of the faithful and the institutional demands of the Vatican; a Catholicism that knows it must never stop listening to the voice of the most humble. That is to say, between the two poles of its existence, more often than not it takes a stance for the people. These features of Brazilian Catholicism have been demonstrated through the ministry of some of the personalities that have formed its leadership. Dom Hélder Câmara is one of the most outstanding examples of this attitude of service to the least privileged.

DOM HÉLDER'S LIFE STORY

Dom Hélder's choice for the "humble" (a term he often used for the poor) was not immediate. In the course of his life, we find him sometimes reaffirming his decisions and sometimes changing and correcting them. These times are "staging posts on life's journey," situations that can help us understand how he defined himself when faced with an existential challenge. I think five steps on his journey are important, five moments that marked the life of Dom Hélder. They help us understand not only the meaning of his existence but above all the ethos by which he lived. Some of these moments occurred when he was already archbishop of Recife, but the impulse that prompted him to define himself was already present at earlier stages in his life.

Priestly calling and prophetic ministry

First, in the person of Dom Hélder priestly calling and prophetic ministry belong together. The former is almost natural, something that developed from early childhood; as he entered adolescence, he also entered the seminary. As a priest, he prepared himself to serve the institution and to administer the sacraments to the people on its behalf. The priest understood that his person had to be at the disposal of the institution and its requirements. The priest saw the world from the standpoint and through the prism of the church. Dom Hélder acknowledged this in his conversations with José de Broucker when he recalled how, on being ordained as a priest in 1931, he was convinced that he was bound by duty to authority and the established order, including the social order.[1] The priest defended the institutional order; he lived to maintain it.

Nevertheless, as he developed, the man who was to be archbishop of Recife gradually became aware that to be a Christian is to be part of a prophetic movement that is open to the future because of the coming kingdom which causes the future to break into our everyday lives. This awareness of being turned toward the future led him to a radical questioning of his relations with the established order. When he was involved in setting up the movement that became the Movimiento de Educación de Base (MEB), an ambitious program of popular education that put the pedagogy of Paulo Freire into practice in adult education projects, Dom Hélder realized that he had to listen to the people. "We have to start from where our people are.... Incarnation means that we have to place ourselves at the level of the people we live and work with—not in order to stay there, obviously, but to help them move forward. But doing this means starting from where our people are."[2] He listened to the people and dreamed of creating the conditions that would allow men and women of the poorest sectors to grow and develop. This listening was something Dom Hélder realized he had to do, especially when he was appointed auxiliary bishop of Rio de Janeiro in the early 1950s. The social change the people want cannot be imposed from the top down. It comes about as the result of action at the grassroots of society. From that time on, prophetic mission was more important to him than the priesthood. This option did not make his life any easier. He had to deal with the established authorities, as well as with incomprehension in the ranks of the church, and even among his fellow bishops. All this testifies to his prophetic quality. Dom Hélder's wisdom lay in going ahead with his mission without breaking his priestly vocation.

National consciousness

Second, this man of the northeast did not stay put within the bounds of his own territory or region. He knew that it was his destiny, as a person and as a minister, to serve his country. Dom Hélder had a strong sense of being Brazilian. This identity was linked to the prophetic dimension of his personality. Hélder was already ordained as a priest when in the 1930s Brazil was shaken by people of diverse tendencies attempting to impose their own beliefs as they sought to forge the destiny of the nation. Hélder Câmara was attracted by the Movimiento Integralista, a

---

[1] Hélder Câmara, *Les conversions d'un évêque: Entretiens avec José de Broucker* (Paris: Éditions du Seuil, 1977), 51.

[2] Ibid., 115.

Brazilian nationalist movement with fascist tendencies, led by Plinio Salgado. During this period in Latin American history, nationalist political groups fighting the imperial powers followed the example of extreme right-wing movements in Europe. Salgado was a charismatic personality who in spite of his obvious power was forced into exile when Getulio Vargas passed a decree outlawing the Movimiento Integralista.

This nationalist phase helped confirm Hélder Câmara's national consciousness, his awareness of belonging to a people that was regarded as a sleeping giant with enormous potential. It is common knowledge that in Latin America, Brazil is the country most likely to become a major power, not only because of the size of its territory and population, but also because of its natural resources and its geographical position. The problem is how to waken the giant, and make him get up and walk. This is where the importance of education comes in. Hélder Câmara had been in charge of the educational work of the Archdiocese of Fortaleza. He was called to a similar task, with much more influence on national life, in the Archdiocese of Rio de Janeiro, and it was there that he discovered the poor. From then on, he gave priority in his life to the humblest sections of society.

In 1955, an international eucharistic congress was held in Rio de Janeiro, and Msgr. Cámara was responsible for organizing it. Two small hillocks near Guanabara Bay were leveled, leaving a vast space where crowds could gather to take part in celebrations of the Eucharist. The problem was that thousands of poor people had lived on these hills; *favelas* (shantytowns) were destroyed when the mounds were removed. Officials offered the inhabitants the chance to go and live in places on the outskirts of Rio, with the idea that this move could reduce the poverty in the region. Msgr. Câmara discovered soon afterward that the result was not a decrease in poverty. Quite the opposite, in fact: the number of those in poverty had grown.

Increasing internal migration yielded the same effect, as more and more people from the rural areas migrated to the cities in search of new opportunities. They headed for São Paulo and Rio de Janeiro, as well as other large urban centers. These poor people were attempting to escape the vicious cycle of poverty, but they found themselves in an even more difficult and hopeless situation.

What was to be done? Msgr. Câmara's experience with social development programs was extremely important here, in that he had an understanding of true popular education. Paulo Freire had launched his pedagogy of liberation in Pernambuco. Following Freire's ideas, Catholic Action, and especially groups of young people had decided to contribute to the transformation of Brazilian society through educational programs that would also rouse the consciousness of the people. In other words, the educators would help create a social awareness that would encourage the adults taking part in these learning experiences to struggle for social change. And so the Movimiento de Educación de Base (MEB) took shape. Many of its militants became politically radical after joining MEB programs as monitors of literacy and culture groups. The "animators" of the literacy-training groups were in turn brought to social awareness by the educators. The educational program opened the door to a much wider project, change in the countries of Latin America.

Organizing the episcopate in Brazil and Latin America

Third, there came a moment on the journey when auxiliary bishop Msgr. Hélder Câmara, a man of great vision and initiative and a talented organizer, became convinced of the need to create a national conference of bishops in Brazil. This step was the result of a dynamic process that started immediately after the Second World War, when the Vatican authorities decided to create many new dioceses in Brazil. Msgr. Câmara saw the importance of an episcopal conference as a forum where the bishops could meet and reflect.

This move was complemented by a further step which Dom Hélder proposed to Msgr. Montini, then secretary of state at the Holy See (subsequently cardinal archbishop of Milan before being elected as the supreme pontiff in 1963). His proposal was to organize the Latin American Episcopal Council, bringing together all the Roman Catholic bishops in Iberian America. So this third moment of Dom Hélder's journey involved organizing the episcopate in Brazil and, beyond that, in the whole of Latin America. Relations among the bishops in the region strengthened and developed during the period of the Second Vatican Council. Mutual confidence was such that when the bishops' conference was held in Medellín in 1968, the guidelines issued for the different ministries of the church took a definite turn towards liberation. It was the Medellín meeting that recognized the Comunidades Eclesiales de Base (CEBs, Church Base Communities) and the theology of liberation. And it was at Medellín that the Latin American Catholic bishops announced their "preferential option for the poor." Dom Hélder, who had been consecrated archbishop of Recife in 1964, was in the forefront of this movement. He was not alone, but on this occasion he was the one to take the decisive step.

Third World Bishops' Manifesto

Fourth, in those times of liberating awareness among many bishops, Dom Hélder played a leading role in the drafting and dissemination of the "Declaration on the Situation of the Third World" (better known as the "Third World Bishops' Manifesto"). This document is crucial to understanding the change of direction that took place among a large section of the Catholic clergy in Latin America, and its influence reached beyond the bounds of the Catholic world. The declaration was acclaimed by many Protestants, and even by atheists and agnostics. The bishops who signed it, seventeen in all, eight of them from Brazil headed by Dom Hélder, based themselves on Paul VI's encyclical *Populorum Progressio*. In March 1967 they announced that they were making a clear choice for the (integral) liberation of the people of the third world which should be reflected in social equality, given that "there can be no peace without justice." The text had repercussions far beyond its own context; for example, it calls for emancipation from the "imperialism of money" which has weighed so heavily on the peoples of the south during the past twenty years. It also expresses fundamental solidarity among the bishops.

It was at this moment in his life (chronologically speaking, before the Medellín meeting) that Dom Hélder recognized that the episcopal ministry has a collegial dimension. Being bishop of Olinda and Recife required him to live in communion not only with the bishops of Brazil, but also with the bishops of the whole church. Among those signing the declaration were Msgr. Angelo Cuniberti, apostolic vicar of Florence, Italy, as well as prelates from China, Indonesia, Lebanon, and elsewhere. The text indicates that the attitude taken by the nonaligned countries (the "Third World") at the Bandung Conference (Indonesia, April 1955) had also spread to the pastors of the Catholic church. The declaration stresses that the bishop's duty is to remain among his people despite any harassment to which he may be subjected by the economic and political powers-that-be. This presence of the pastor among his people, sharing in the cry of the oppressed, signals the demand for the protection of human dignity, social justice, equality between the classes, and the common good.

The bishops' document continues with a theological reflection along the lines of Latin American liberation theology, according to which "theology is a second act" (a term used by Gustavo Gutiérrez). Their reflection includes a reference to the Qur'an, testifying to the ecumenical spirit of the document. The document ends on a prophetic note by reminding governments that the role of the state is not to impose itself by force, but to put an end to the class struggle by establishing justice.

Hidden discipleship
Fifth, although Dom Hélder Câmara himself was reluctant to talk about this point, one element runs like a red thread through all his mutations.

In his conversations with José de Broucker he called it "hidden discipleship"; it was the spiritual practice of a small group of people who met to meditate and pray together.[3] Hidden discipleship meant, above all, learning to be humble—a path similar to that proposed by Dietrich Bonhoeffer when he wrote about "the discipline of the arcane." This spiritual practice is essential to maintaining integrity and constancy for any who wish to follow Jesus. This element was perhaps present from the beginning of the life of Dom Hélder Câmara.

THE PUBLIC DIMENSION OF DOM HÉLDER'S LIFE

The historical period in which Hélder Câmara lived was far from placid. These were turbulent years, when violent social and political struggles followed one another in quick succession. Brazil went through a long period when everything was dominated by the need for the country to build itself as a nation. The nation in turn had to meet the challenge of social, economic, political, and cultural modernization. We have already seen how Msgr. Câmara was involved in popular education programs first in his native Ceará and later in other undertakings on a national scale. His pastoral commitment gradually made him aware of the needs of the poorest sectors of Brazil's population. This awareness in turn prompted him to set up human advancement programs in the area of Rio de Janeiro, where he was auxiliary bishop, and then in the Archdiocese of Olinda and Recife where he became archbishop in 1964. During those years, forces trying to seize power at the national level clashed bitterly. Violence indelibly marked Brazil's political life at that time. Getulio Vargas was elected president in 1950 and tensions grew during his term in office. His suicide in August 1954 was a tragic event that highlighted the crisis affecting Brazil. It marked the beginning of a period of political turmoil, ending in an election won by Juscelino Kubitschek.

For a few years, the new president managed to create a sense that Brazil was getting over its most serious problems. This period saw the building of the new federal capital, Brasilia, inaugurated in 1960. Industrialization was also progressing. However, when Janio Quadros took over the presidency from Kubitschek, social tensions resurfaced. Quadros resigned in 1961, and vice president Joao Goulart was unable to handle the situation. Some people were trying to develop social welfare programs launched by the government, while others reacted against the prospect of change. This was the situation when, at the end of March 1964, the armed forces staged a coup d'état, which marked the beginning

---

[3] Ibid., 99–104.

of almost two decades of military governments imposing national security regimes in most countries in Latin America and the Caribbean.

Some people who believed in social progress maintained that structural change was possible in the countries of Latin America. The Cuban revolution had been in progress since early 1959, and inspired by this, the most dynamic and idealistic elements among Latin American youth had embarked on revolutionary action. The military in power responded with violence: imprisonment, torture, exile, disappearances, abductions, and killings were regular occurrences during those turbulent years. Young people in the churches were no exception. In Brazil, for example, the repression severely affected Catholic Youth Action, especially its student groups, which became more and more radical. The same kind of movement was going on throughout Latin America and in this context Latin American liberation theology began to take shape.

Most political parties bowed to the power of the military. The trades unions were persecuted; a few let themselves be used, and the ones pressing for social progress were disbanded. The press was systematically censored. Terror stalked the streets. Any who dared to disagree with the military dictators were threatened with reprisals. In the face of these reactionary methods, the people seemed paralyzed; they did not know what to do or where to turn. When all the spaces where they might have assembled were closed to them, they began timidly to realize that there were places where those who had no right to speak could at least whisper their disagreement and protest. Among those places were some churches whose authorities were sympathetic and prepared to show solidarity with the people in their distress. These spaces became a refuge for those attempting to oppose the injustices done by national security military regimes.

At this time, Dom Hélder Câmara acquired enormous stature as a public figure. A small man with a tremendous vision, a pastor of the church and a member of its hierarchy, he did not oppose the dictators on the grounds of political party. He was led into opposition by the convictions that had developed in the course of the mutations described above. During these years of terror imposed by force of arms, the prophet's voice resounded in the midst of an oppressive silence. As in ancient Israel the prophets proclaimed their visions in faithfulness to Yahweh, often in opposition to the king, Dom Hélder did not stay silent. He simply bore witness to what he knew. He said, among other things, that the "revolution" led by the military was increasing social injustice rather than alleviating it, that the poor now lived with more fear and less hope. He stated aloud what many people knew but did not have the courage to say, namely that those in power were repressing civil liberties and that their reactionary violence reached its climax in the use of torture and the killing of social activists. His voice rang out loud and clear in the surrounding silence.

The military responded swiftly. First, all mention of him was suppressed. His writings and his thoughts could not be diffused by the media. The authorities even went so far as to say that he could not be mentioned in a mass of the seventh day, sometimes celebrated in the Catholic church in memory of a person who has died. Then he was harassed by other means, including a particularly vile attack in the form of the murder of one of his closest collaborators in the Archdiocese of Olinda and Recife. The body of Father Henrique Pereira Neto was found hanging from a tree in the square outside the episcopal residence.

Despite all the efforts of the apparatus of repression, Dom Hélder's standing as a public figure grew and he acquired national and international stature. People conscious of the need for democracy called on him for help and guidance. Many students, braving censorship and repression, invited him to meetings and university graduation ceremonies. These activities led to a new campaign of repression against him and to still greater hostility. He was not supposed to speak in public, but he continued nevertheless to bear witness to the truth. He did so in terms of the gospel, calling for repentance and reconciliation, which he regarded as essential for rebuilding national life. The roots of this attitude are to be found in the transformation of his life and thinking after he turned away from the integrist movement headed by Plinio Salgado. After this unfortunate excursion, Msgr. Câmara, like other Brazilian Catholics, realized that his nationalism had to be tempered by Christian humanism. To put it another way, the human being for whose redemption God gave himself in Jesus Christ must always be the focus of concern for every citizen, and for the state and the church.

Because of these convictions, Dom Hélder was not satisfied with technical solutions aimed at triggering processes of development. Development is not only economic; it extends to all aspects of life. Consequently, in his view, development has to be accompanied by liberation, which happens concretely when human beings succeed in overcoming their narrow limitations and are able to love God and their neighbor. He often commented with respect on the position of atheist humanists who show love for their neighbor who is the victim of injustice. But he insisted that love for the neighbor is only half of the love we have to show. We have to set ourselves free to love God. But he would go on to say that anyone who says they love God without loving their neighbor has not experienced the total freedom offered by the gospel. The point he was making is important for Christians and atheists, believers and agnostics alike. When the human being is the focus of our attention, technical solutions aiming to improve human living conditions are welcome, but they are not enough. Something more is needed, and that something is love, especially love for the poor and oppressed.

Driven by this gospel love, Dom Hélder lived his life in the service of the poor. Because of this love, he was faithful to the truth when censorship sought to suppress it. Imbued with this love, he decided to take part in international campaigns for human development and for the defense and enforcement of human rights. This love caused him to join the struggle for agrarian reform in North-East Brazil, to make church properties available to landless peasants. And above all, this knowledge of the gospel's love caused him to opt for active nonviolence in an epoch in the history of Latin America (and of the world) that was characterized by violence and the use of force. It took great integrity and courage to make this decision. At that time in Vietnam, the USA was making war on a people in quest of emancipation and national identity. The violence used by the aggressor was inexcusable. Many people thought that the struggle of the Vietnamese was legitimate in every respect. Dom Hélder, on the other hand, believed with great humility that Gandhi and Martin Luther King had set the path of liberation.[4]

He used this nonviolent approach in confronting the military who were governing Brazil. The repressors used force. Dom Hélder Câmara and those around him chose the path of resistance without violence. At first, his option profoundly shocked those who were engaged in the armed struggle, or were sympathetic to it. However, his vision gradually won over many people who were opposed to the national security regime and had been ready to join the armed struggle to fight against the military. It was a long but fruitful road, and his nonviolent approach was greeted with enthusiasm by many far beyond the lands in the American hemisphere south of the Río Bravo.

For a large segment of public opinion, Dom Hélder was above all a visionary. But though he attached great importance to the ultimate purpose of action (what the Greeks called the *telos*), he was always aware that to achieve a goal and press your convictions you have to be organized. In other words, we have to set a path between the point at which we find ourselves and the goal we want to reach. This is the path of liberation. Msgr. Câmara knew that this path could be pioneered by small groups, communities that could act in the service of the mass of the population. The people who form such minorities, Dom Hélder said, belong to the family of Abraham, so he called them "Abrahamic

---

[4] See Hélder Câmara, *Spiral of Violence* (London: Sheed and Ward, 1971).

minorities." Like Abraham they are moved by faith, by the courage to live and continue to live according to God's will. He saw these Abrahamic minorities more as organisms than as organizations, as more concerned with the spirit than the institution, with life style rather than with organization. For these groups, the most important thing should be looking at and understanding the situation, listening to those who suffer, and committing themselves along with their brothers and sisters in the Abrahamic community to be faithful to God's will in the world.[5]

In Dom Hélder's understanding, while social transformation programs must benefit the masses, they are actually the result of the hard work and commitment of small groups of people cooperating in movements that are trying to do something to improve the lot of the majorities. Msgr Câmara never perceived the Abrahamic minorities as elite groups. Consequently, in his ministry as archbishop of Recife he gave high priority to forming the Movement of Brothers. The name is significant; these groups are on the move, trying to bring change in the situations in which they are involved. What prompts them to act is love. So they express the fellowship that unites them and they practice love among themselves, in the hope that others in society will also be infected by it.

WHAT REMAINS OF THE LIFE AND WORK OF DOM HÉLDER CÂMARA?

The administration of church institutions is often surprising. Sometimes when pastors end their ministry, other leaders succeed them, who differ from their predecessors in character and life style. The impression is that the tendency in the chain of leadership is to introduce elements that will change the institution.

When Dom Hélder reached the age of retirement, the person called to replace him was a hierarch specializing in canon law. So the handing over of responsibility came as a shock; it was strange and unexpected choice. In other words, the prophet was succeeded by the lawyer, the visionary by someone whose primary concern would be institutional forms. The change of tone in the administration of the Archdiocese of Olinda and Recife was felt immediately. In Dom Hélder's time, for example, peasants who wanted to meet and consult the archbishop about their problems were attended to at once. After he retired, they were practically ignored by the new authorities. There was no question now of applying the preferential option for the poor. At another level, the Theological Institute of Recife, an institution that had been in the vanguard of theological education, was rapidly dismantled.

---

[5] Hélder Câmara, *The Desert Is Fertile* (New York: Orbis Bks., 1974), 54ff.

Msgr. Câmara continued to receive invitations to address many groups and different types of audiences, but not in Recife. His pastoral work was reduced to ruins. What remained was a sense of absence, the nostalgia we feel when someone is no longer there, and which evokes a presence that is stronger than the absence. This is not the longing we feel for someone who has died, but rather a feeling that makes us turn toward someone who is still present with us as a life force that inspires and guides us, and confirms the faith of the believers, especially the humble. We look to a presence that helps keep hope alive through the witness of love he bore by his existence.

Hélder Câmara was a personality who left his mark on the work of Vatican II and stamped the evolution of the churches' life after the council. That stamp is ecumenical. Although profoundly Catholic and faithful to the Roman institution, his vision included an ecumenism in which an ecclesia free of confessional distinctions would open the way to the future. Here again, in this person so full of life we see combined the gifts of prophet and priest.

If I speak in the name of God and the poor
I cannot be against progress.
When I see how much the human mind
has already invented and manufactured
to deliver women and men from cold and hunger,
from pain, sickness, and suffering,
from ignorance, from isolation, and so on,
I have to say: we must go on.
There is still far too much hunger, pain,
disease, ignorance, and solitude.

Human beings, God's co-creators,
still have a great deal to do to finish and perfect creation,
the mission they have received from the Lord.

And so I say to you:
let us walk courageously, daringly, along the road of progress.
But let us be careful not to crush anyone,
not to leave anyone lying in the ditch.
The progress we have to make first, then,
may not be in our super-laboratories and super-factories.
It may have to be made in our minds and hearts.
What I mean is that it will have to be made
in our appetite for and will to progress.
Progress for what? For what kind of growth? For whose profit?
There is no truly human progress
without progress in social awareness, social conscience.

Dom Hélder Câmara
Questions for Living

2 | *Dom Hélder Câmara's concern for the poor*
Toward a humane world order with sustainable development and human rights

KAMAL HOSSAIN

D om Hélder Câmara exemplified in his life profound concern for the injustice suffered by the poor. His thought and actions inspired women and men to dream and hope for liberation, and to believe in the strength inherent in them to liberate themselves and their societies. The lectures I delivered as Dom Hélder Câmara Visiting Professor at the Free University of Amsterdam in 1997 focused on universal human rights providing core values as a basis for building as humane a world order as could be built.

Dom Hélder Câmara's approach to social justice was derived from a profound respect for the human person. It was in his native land of Brazil that the 1992 United Nations Conference on Environment and Development ("the Rio Conference") adopted by consensus the Rio Declaration, which declared that human beings are central to the concerns for sustainable development. The basic goal of sustainable human development is to enable all people to live in freedom and with dignity, which pervasive poverty denies them.

The failure of earlier policies to eradicate poverty originated in the incapacity of the policy discourse to address the challenge presented by existing disparities of power and wealth within and among nations and thereby to find a place for justice in development. Injustice is institutionalized in social, political, legal, and economic structures of

Kamal Hossain was the Dom Hélder Câmara Professor of the Free University of Amsterdam in 1997. He also is a barrister-at-law, and a senior advocate, Supreme Court of Bangladesh. Other positions he holds, or has held, are chairman of the Committee on Legal Aspects of Sustainable Development, International Law Association; chairman of the Advisory Group for Transparency International; director of the International Centre for Human Rights and Democratic Development (Canada); and visiting fellow, All Souls College, Oxford.

societies. These institutions contribute to the polarization in societies between a narrow elite and the deprived majority, as well as between men and women, which reflects the injustices that pervade many societies.

As the World Bank's World Development Report 2000/2001 confirms, the world has deep poverty amid plenty. Of the world's 6 billion people, 2.8 billion—almost half—live on less than $2 a day, and 1.2 billion—a fifth—live on less than $1 a day. Forty-four percent live in South Asia, where I come from. In rich countries, the mortality rate for children under five is less than one in a hundred, while in the poorest countries as many as a one child in five does not reach its fifth birthday. And while in rich countries less than 5 percent of all children under five are malnourished, in poor countries as many as 50 percent are. This destitution persists although human conditions have improved more in the past century than in the rest of history; global wealth, global connections, and technological capabilities have never been greater. But the distribution of these global gains is extraordinarily unequal. The report goes on to diagnose: "In a world where political power is unequally distributed and often mimics the distribution of economic power, the way state institutions operate may be particularly unfavourable to poor people. For example, poor people frequently do not receive the benefits of public investment in education and health. And they are often the victims of corruption and arbitrariness on the part of the state."

FROM STOCKHOLM TO RIO: THE EMERGENCE OF THE CONCEPT OF SUSTAINABLE DEVELOPMENT

As we stand at the beginning of the twenty-first century, we need to sharpen our focus on the outstanding legal issues that confront the international community. The quest continues for a normative order effectively addressing vital concerns of the global economy and the global environment. International law on these matters has undergone progressive development, and the time has come to take stock in order to identify the issues.

The 1972 Stockholm Declaration of the United Nations Conference on the Human Environment provided a basis for increasing awareness of environmental issues, and its seminal role was assessed thus:

> *Notwithstanding its non-binding character, the Stockholm Declaration is generally regarded as the foundation of modern international environmental law. Despite its ambiguities, the Declaration eventually acquired not only moral and political value, but some of the principles laid down in it are now considered as part and parcel of general international law and as binding on*

governments, independent of their specific consent. In particular, Principle 21 has evolved into hard law.... The Stockholm Declaration has served as a basis for the subsequent development of international environmental law in the form of numerous bilateral and multilateral conventions and other legally binding instruments.[1]

The initial linkage of development and environment in international legal discourse is generally attributed to the Stockholm Declaration, endorsed by the United Nations General Assembly. That declaration had recognized that "both aspects of man's environment, the natural and the man-made, are essential to his well being and to the enjoyment of basic human rights—even the right to life itself."[2]

The efforts of developing countries to secure recognition of development as a right with correlative legal duties and responsibilities led to the United Nations Declaration on the Right to Development (adopted by United Nations General Assembly, Resolution No. 41/128, 4 December 1986). The declaration focused on the human person as the central subject of development. It sought to base the international obligation both of states and of the international community to promote development on the universal recognition accorded to the basic human rights of all people (Article 1). It also identified important elements that ought to be embraced by the concept of development: equality of opportunity for all in their access to basic resources, education, health services, food, housing, employment, and fair distribution of income; ensuring an active role for women in the development process; adoption of economic and social reforms to remove social injustices; and encouragement of popular participation in all spheres relating to development.

The linkage between the natural and "man-made" environment was thus restated in the UN Declaration on the Right to Development, which reaffirmed the responsibility of the international community and of states for sustained action to promote more rapid development of developing countries. It was asserted that "as a complement to the efforts of developing countries, effective international cooperation is essential in providing these countries with appropriate means and facilities to foster their comprehensive development."[3] The concept of

---

[1] Marc Pallemaerts, "International Environmental Law from Stockholm to Rio: Back to the Future?" in *Greening International Law,* ed. Philippe Sands (London: Earthscan Pubns., 1993), 2.

[2] "Declaration of the United Nations Conference on the Human Environment," Stockholm, Sweden, 5–16 June 1972.

[3] Article 4, "United Nations Declaration on the Right to Development," adopted by United Nations General Assembly, Resolution 41/128, 4 December 1986.

development was elucidated in the following terms: "Development is a comprehensive economic, social, cultural and political process, which aims at the constant improvement and the well-being of the entire population and of all individuals on the basis of their active, free and meaningful participation in development and in the fair distribution of benefits resulting therefrom."[4]

Development is thus viewed as centering around the human person, and the international obligation to promote development is seen as being derived from the obligation to respect universally recognized human rights. The interrelatedness of development and human rights was emphasized thus: "All human rights and fundamental freedoms are indivisible and interdependent," and "states should take steps to eliminate obstacles to development resulting from failure to observe civil and political rights as well as economic, social and cultural rights."[5]

The United Nations had taken a major initiative in response to growing concerns regarding environment and development by establishing (pursuant to a United Nations General Assembly [UNGA] Resolution) a World Commission on Environment and Development, named the Brundtland Commission because it was chaired by Mrs. Gro Harlem Brundtland, then leader of the Norwegian Labour Party. The Brundtland Report, *Our Common Future* (1987), underscored the linkage between development and environment and called for the adoption globally of a strategy of sustainable development, which was defined as "development that meets the needs of the present without compromising the ability of future generations to meet their own needs."[6] The report not only reaffirmed the basic premise of the Declaration on the Right to Development that the human person is the central subject of development, but gave a new salience to the issues of equity and, in particular, intergenerational equity.

The Brundtland Commission urged the drawing up of a "Universal Declaration" and later a "Convention on Environmental Protection and Sustainable Development." The Expert Group on Environmental Law (set up by the commission with a mandate to formulate legal principles that ought to be put in place immediately or before 2000 to support environmental protection and sustainable development) presented a consolidated report setting out its formulation in twenty-two articles

---

[4] Ibid., preamble.

[5] Ibid., preamble, Article 6.

[6] *Our Common Future,* The Report of the World Commission on Environment and Development (Oxford: WCED, 1987), 5–6.

under the title, Legal Principles for Environmental Protection and Sustainable Development.

The Brundtland Report focused on the critical link between development and environment.

> *Ecology and economy are becoming even more interwoven—locally, regionally, nationally, and globally—into a seamless net of causes and effects.... Impoverishing the local resource base can impoverish wider areas. Deforestation by highland farmers causes flooding on lowland farms: factory pollution robs local fishermen of their catch. Such local cycles now operate nationally and regionally. Dryland deforestation sends environmental refugees in their millions across national borders. Deforestation in Latin America and Asia is causing more floods in downhill, downstream nations. Acid precipitation and nuclear fallout spread across the borders of Europe. Similar phenomena are emerging on a global scale as the loss of ozone. Internationally traded hazardous chemicals entering goods are themselves internationally traded.... Over the past few decades, life threatening environmental concerns have surfaced in the developing world.... Yet these developing countries must operate in a world in which the resources gap between most developing and industrialized countries dominates in the rule making of some key international bodies, and in which the industrialized world has already used much of the planet's main "environment" resources; this is also its main "development problem."*[7]

The General Assembly in 1989 by its Resolution 44/228 decided to convene the United Nations Conference on Environment and Development in 1992. The crucial challenge of the conference, that of fully and indissolubly integrating environment and development because "development and environment must be one"[8] is reflected in the declared objectives of the conference as set out in the UNGA resolution, which include the following:

> *To examine the relationship between environmental degradation and the international economic environment, with a view to ensuring a more integrated approach to problems of environment and development in relevant international forums without introducing new forms of conditionality;*

> *To examine strategies for national and international action with a view to arriving at specific agreements and commitments by Governments and by intergovernmental organizations for defined activities to promote a supportive international economic climate conducive to sustained and environmentally sound development in all countries, with a view to combating poverty and improving the quality of life, and bearing in mind that the incorporation of*

---

[7] Ibid.

[8] *The Challenge of the Environment* (United Nations Development Program, 1991), 3.

environmental concerns and considerations in development planning and policies should not be used to introduce new forms of conditionality in aid or in development financing and should not serve as a pretext for creating unjustified barriers to trade.[9]

The concept of sustainable development was introduced in the World Conservation Strategy (1980). The concept emerged in the context of conservation of natural resources, but contained within it wider implications, extending from human rights and governance issues to those involving the functioning of the international economy and national development strategies. The Brundtland Report identified some of these elements and added depth to the concept of sustainable development. The Rio Declaration thus marked the culmination of a process that went back at least twenty years to the Stockholm Declaration of 1972.

THE RIO DECLARATION: A FRAMEWORK FOR PROGRESSIVE DEVELOPMENT OF EMERGING INTERNATIONAL LEGAL NORMS ON SUSTAINABLE DEVELOPMENT

The Declaration of the United Nations Conference on Environment and Development (UNCED), held in Rio de Janeiro in June 1992, ("the Rio Declaration") enunciated twenty-seven principles, proclaiming as its objectives the establishing of a new and equitable global partnership through the creation of new levels of cooperation among states and key sectors of society and people. It was envisaged that this partnership would work toward international agreements that respect the interest of all and protect the integrity of the global environment and developmental system. The declaration recognized the integral and interdependent nature of the earth, our home, and enunciated as the first principle, "Human beings are at the centre of concerns for sustainable development. Furthermore, they are entitled to a healthy and productive life in harmony with nature." Adopted with the declaration was Agenda 21, an 800-page document embodying guidelines for future national and international action in the field of environment and development.

The concept of sustainable development thus reflects a number of the core values and normative prescriptions that had been earlier embodied in the Seoul Declaration and in the Declaration on the Right to Development. Satisfying human needs, present and future, is made the basic objective of development. Global disparities call for application of equitable principles to ensure meeting the basic needs of all. A global strategy for promoting growth is urged which would entail adopting an integrated approach recognizing the linkages between natural resources,

---

[9] United Nations General Assembly, Resolution 44/228, 22 December 1989.

financial resources, technology, and the operation of institutions at the national and international level.

The Rio Declaration has been described "as an international instrument of general principles and obligations which was negotiated in detail by a large and representative number of delegations and must be taken to reflect—to the extent any international instrument can do so— the current consensus of values and priorities in environment and development."[10] Its critical significance has been noted to be that it reflects "a major paradigm shift from international environmental law to a new (and yet to be defined) law of sustainable development."[11] Principle 22 calls for "further development of international law in the field of sustainable development."

The new international law on sustainable development would thus not only comprise rules of law which were hitherto understood to constitute international environmental law, but also integrate with it elements of what hitherto has been described as "international development law." The provisions of Chapter 39 of Agenda 21 are that further development of international law on sustainable development will have to pay "special attention to the delicate balance between environment and development concerns," and calls for effective participation by all countries concerned in reviewing both the past performance and effectiveness of existing international instruments and institutions as well as priorities for future law-making on sustainable development. This may include, in the language of Chapter 39, "an examination of the feasibility of elaborating general rights and obligations of States, as appropriate, in the field of sustainable development."

The progress of international law on sustainable development must begin with an elucidation of the concept of sustainable development. The growing body of literature underlines the multidimensional character of the concept on sustainable development. The Stockholm Declaration itself had recognized the importance of both aspects of environment, "the natural" and the "[hu]man-made." The Club of Rome's latest report describes a sustainable society not only in terms of physical sustain-ability but in terms of one based on social justice. "A sustainable society implicitly connotes one that is based on a long-term vision in that it must foresee the consequences of its diverse activities to ensure that they do

---

[10] Ileana Porras, "The Rio Declaration: A New Basis for International Cooperation," in *Greening International Law*, ed. Sands, 21.

[11] Peter H. Sand, "International Environmental Law after Rio," *European Journal for International Law* 4 (1993): 378.

not break the cycles of renewal; it has to be a society of conservation and generational concern. It must avoid the adoption of mutually irreconcilable objectives. Equally, it must be a society of social justice because great disparities of wealth or privilege will breed destructive disharmony."[12]

Ben Boer's study, "Implementing Sustainability in Developing Countries,"[13] draws on a variety of sources to elucidate the multidimensional character of the concept. It draws on a subsequent elaboration of the concept by Mrs. Brundtland herself as exemplified in the following terms: "There are many dimensions to sustainability. First, it requires the elimination of poverty and deprivation. Second, it requires the conservation and enhancement of the resources base which alone can ensure that the elimination of poverty is permanent. Third, it requires a broadening of the concept of development so that it covers not only economic growth but also social and cultural development. Fourth, and most important, it requires the unification of economics and ecology in decision-making at all levels."

A Canadian government document cited by Boer suggests that to be sustainable, development must meet three fundamental and equal objectives:

1. *an economic objective: the production of goods and services. The overriding criterion in fulfilling this objective is efficiency;*

2. *an environment objective: the conservation and prudent management of natural resources. The overriding criterion here is the preservation of biodiversity and maintenance of biological integrity;*

3. *a social objective: the maintenance and enhancement of the equality of life. Equity is the main consideration in meeting this objective.*

The need for a new framework in which to promote global development and protect the global environment is underlined in these studies and the concept of sustainable development is put forward as an overriding global objective to be secured by the universal acceptance of new principles and rules.

Key elements of the concept are spelled out by the Brundtland Report.

a. *The concept of sustainable development does imply limits—not absolute limits but limitations imposed by the present state of technology and*

---

[12] Alexander King, *The First Global Revolution,* Report by the Council of the Club of Rome (New York: Simon & Schuster, 1991), 49.

[13] Ben Boer, "Implementing Sustainability in Developing Countries" (paper presented at the Lawasia Conference on Environmental Law, Bangkok, 1991).

social organization and environmental resources and by the ability of the biosphere to absorb the effect of human activities.

b.   *Sustainable development requires meeting the basic needs of all and extending to all the opportunity to fulfill their aspirations for a better life.... A world in which poverty is endemic will always be prone to ecological and other catastrophes.*

c.   *Meeting essential needs requires not only a new era of economic growth for nations in which the majority are poor, but an assurance that those poor get their full share of the resources required to attain that growth.*

d.   *Such equity would be aided by political systems that secure effective citizen participation in decision-making and by greater democracy in international decision-making.*

e.   *Sustainable development requires that those who are more affluent adopt lifestyles within the planet's ecological means in their use of energy; for example, rapidly growing populations can increase the pressure on resources.*

f.   *Sustainable development is not a fixed state of harmony but rather a process of change in which the exploitation of resources, the divesting of investments, the orientation of technological development and institutional change are made consistent with future as well as present needs.*[14]

UNITED NATIONS CONFERENCE ON THE ENVIRONMENT AND DEVELOPMENT, THE GLOBAL ECONOMY, AND INTERNATIONAL ECONOMIC RELATIONS

Inherent in the concept of sustainable development is the tension between the competing goals of environmental protection and economic development, and in an international community made up of disparate groups of states, the tension between the goals of developed and developing states. As a recent study notes, "The earth is under a two-fold attack from human beings—the excessive demands and wasteful habits of affluent populations of developed countries, and the billions of new mouths born in the developing world who (very naturally) aspire to increase their own consumption levels."[15] It is estimated that "about one quarter of the world's population (mostly in the industrial countries) account for about three-quarters of the world's net annual consumption of resources of all kinds. The industrial world consumes 75% of the world's commercial energy, 90% of the world's traded hard wood, 81%

---

[14] *Our Common Future,* 8-9.

[15] Paul M. Kennedy, *Preparing for the Twenty-first Century* (New York: Random Hse., Inc., 1993), 23.

of its paper, 80% of its iron and steel, 70% of its milk and meat, 60% of its fertilizer. The other three-quarters of the world's people must get by together on the remaining one quarter of the resources."[16] On one estimate, every child born in the "North" consumes during a lifetime twenty to thirty times the resources and accounts for twenty to thirty times the waste—year in and year out—of a counterpart in a developing country. The world's population is expected to increase from more than 6 billion people today to 10 billion or more by the middle of the next century—with most of the growth in the poorest regions of the world. This increase will "result in a growing mismatch between where the world's riches, technology, good health and other benefits are to be found and where the world's fast growing new generations possessing few if any of those benefits live. A population explosion on one part of the globe and a technology explosion on the other is not a good recipe for a stable international order."[17]

The challenge before the United Nations Conference on the Environment and Development (UNCED) was to achieve a "global bargain" which would enable the developed and developing countries to reach consensus on a strategy to realize their respective objectives. The essence of the strategy would involve the forging of a "global partnership" under which the developed countries would commit themselves (a) to reduce the burden they impose on the carrying capacity of the earth's eco-system, (b) to alter their existing production and consumption patterns, and (c) to support developing countries in their efforts to adopt and implement new strategies of sustainable development. Developing countries could only make their full contribution to that goal within a framework of effective cooperation between developed and developing countries with such cooperation to include:

a.   *increased access to the markets of the industrialized countries;*

b.   *increased flow of private investment and technology transfer to developing countries;*

c.   *durable solution of the debt problems of the developing countries;*

d.   *substantial external support—financial flows, in particular—to the developing countries.*

---

[16] Shridath Ramphal, "Where Is the Time-Bomb Ticking?" in *Population and Global Security,* ed. Nicholas Polunin (Cambridge: Cambridge Univ.Pr., 1998), 79–92.

[17] Kennedy, *Preparing for the Twenty-first Century,* 331.

These recommendations echo some of the concerns that had prompted the tabling of the New International Economic Order (NIEO) proposals in the seventies.

The UNCED Secretariat estimated that some US $600 billion a year would be required to implement Agenda 21 in the developing countries, the bulk of it to be contributed by the developing countries themselves. The international concessional financing requirement was estimated at US $125 billion. These magnitudes would not appear to be impossibly large if significant reductions of military expenditure could be achieved in a post–Cold War world. Robert McNamara squarely addressed this challenge at a recent international conference: "As we move towards a system providing for collective action against military aggression wherever it may occur, military budgets throughout—in both developed and developing countries—can be reduced substantially. They now total nearly US $1 trillion per year. I believe that during this decade that amount...including expenditure in the developing countries...could be cut in half. The huge savings of approximately 500 billion dollars a year could be used to address the pressing human and physical infrastructure needs across the globe."[18]

The linkage between environment and international economic relations was reflected in the opening address at UNCED by its secretary general.

> The concentration of population growth in developing countries and economic growth in the industrialised countries has deepened, creating imbalances which are unsustainable, either in environmental or economic terms....
> Sustainable development—development that does not destroy or undermine the ecological, economic or social basis on which continued development depends—is the only viable pathway to a more secure and hopeful future for rich and poor alike. Fortunately, that pathway is still an option but that option is closing. This Conference must establish the foundations for effecting the transition to sustainable development. This can only be done through fundamental changes in our economic life and in international economic relations, particularly as between industrialised and developing countries. Environment must be integrated into every aspect of our economic policy and decision-making as well as the culture and value systems which motivate economic behaviour.[19]

The integral link between economy and ecology at the global level and the imperative of international cooperation to achieve sustainable

---

[18] Robert McNamara, "Towards a Non-Violent World Order," (paper presented at the International Conference on Re-defining the Good Society, New Delhi, 1993), 14.

[19] The Earth Summit: The United Nations Conference on Environment and Development (London: Graham & Trotman, 1993), 4.

development were recognized in the seminal work, *Earth in the Balance*, authored by Albert Gore, then incumbent vice president of the United States. Gore writes, "Human civilization is now so complex and diverse, so sprawling and massive that it is difficult to see how we can respond in a co-ordinated, collective way...to the global environmental crisis.... We must find a way to join this common cause. The crisis we face is, in the final analysis, a global problem and can only be solved on a global basis. Merely addressing one dimension or another or trying to implement solutions in only one region of the world or another will, in the end, create frustration, failure, and the weakening of the resolve needed to address the whole of the problem."[20]

He proceeded to urge the need for a global Marshall Plan, conceptually similar to the global partnership that UNCED aimed to promote. "The scope and complexity of this plan will far exceed those of the original; what's required now is a plan that combines large-scale, long-term, carefully targeted financial aid to developing nations, massive efforts to design and then transfer to poor nations the new technologies needed for sustained economic progress, a worldwide program to stabilize world population, and binding commitments by the industrial nations to accelerate their own transition to an environmentally responsible pattern of life."[21]

The objective of such a plan would be to promote sustainable development on a global scale. According to Gore,

> The new global economy must be an inclusive system that does not leave entire regions behind—as our present system leaves out most of Africa and much of Latin America. In an inclusive economy, for instance, wealthy nations can no longer insist that Third World countries pay huge sums of interest on old debts even when the sacrifices necessary to pay them increase the pressure on their suffering populations so much that revolutionary tensions build uncontrollably. The Marshall Plan took the broadest possible view of Europe's problems and developed strategies to serve human need and promote sustained economic progress; we must now do the same on a global scale.[22]

SUSTAINABLE DEVELOPMENT AND HUMAN RIGHTS: SOUTH ASIAN EXPERIENCE

Development strategies devised by the authoritarian regimes in South Asia, without popular participation, have been found to be insensitive to

---

[20] Albert Gore, *Earth in the Balance: Ecology and the Human Spirit* (New York: Plume, 1993), 294.

[21] Ibid., 297.

[22] Ibid., 22.

their human rights implications and wider social impact. Thus the integrated agricultural development program adopted in Nepal in the seventies aimed at increasing agricultural productivity improved the condition of wealthier farmers but by-passed small farmers and agricultural laborers.[23] The experience in Bangladesh in the eighties was similar; there an evaluation of the Integrated Rural Development Program found that

> *differential access to credit and other inputs among the IRDP membership resulted in both a more dramatic differentiation among those with and without access to the HYV [High Yielding Varieties] package and, as importantly, land consolidation and land fragmentation. Landholding patterns became more and more skewed among the membership in concert with differential access to resources.... The takeover by larger farmers of rural inputs and initially innovative development programmes has enhanced and stimulated the process of inequality already in operation. Rather than generate a climate in which all rural producers were encouraged and able to enhance their productive capacity, the Green Revolution, and the implementation of the IRDP, served to heighten the disparities among rural poor.*[24]

The stringent adjustment programs forced on many developing countries under authoritarian regimes resulted in economic stagnation and indiscipline (as reflected in the decade of the eighties), and have exacted high economic and social costs. Conventional adjustment policy "transmits and usually multiplies the impact on the poor and the vulnerable." As shown in many countries, the result is rising malnutrition. Thus it is argued that to neglect

> *the human dimension of adjustment is not only a human tragedy; it is an economic error of the most fundamental sort. Much evidence already exists of the economic returns to investment in human resources. To fail to protect young children at the critical stages of their growth and development is to wreak lasting damage on a whole generation, the results of which may well have effects on economic development and welfare for decades ahead. Moreover, in the short run, it is plainly absurd to imagine that economic dynamism can be fully restored when an important fraction of a country's workers remain malnourished.... There comes a point beyond—or rather, below—which the cutbacks (on consumption expenditure) and reductions of an adjustment*

---

[23] David Seddon, *Nepal: A State of Poverty* (New Delhi: Vikas Publishing Hse., 1987), 55–61.

[24] Evaluation report by Feldman and McCarthy, cited in A. Z. M. Obaidullah Khan, *Creative Development* (Dhaka: Univ. Pr., 1990), 48.

process become absurdly counter productive to the economic process, let alone to the political and human viability of a country.[25]

The devastating floods of 1988 in Bangladesh generated serious discussions not only in the country but internationally on alternative flood protection strategies. A discussion forum organized by the Bangladesh Agricultural Research Council produced a report underlining the need to take social and environmental dimensions into account when designing flood control structures. Thus it pointed out that fish, which was the major if not the only source of protein for the children of the poor, had already been drastically reduced as a result of constructing polders and embankments. If this trend were to continue, many fish and aquatic plant species could be lost altogether. It gave examples of major irrigation projects that had left many fishing villages in decay because of the resultant lack of employment in the fisheries sector. The report urged that a sustainable flood protection strategy should take into account the agronomic, social, economic, and environmental effects of water control structures on other flood plain components such as fisheries and forestry, as well as the differential impact of flooding on different categories of farmers.

A landmark judgment delivered by the appellate division in 1997 held that an Association of Environmental Lawyers had standing to present a writ petition in the public interest to raise questions regarding the legal validity of a flood action plan prepared without any participation of concerned and affected persons. Such a flood action plan threatened to affect adversely the lives and livelihood of substantial sections of people and to have adverse environmental and ecological effects. The chief justice, after citing the Brundtland Report and Principles 3 and 10 of the Rio Principles, delivered this leading judgment: "In this context of emerging concern for the conservation of environment, irrespective of the locality where it is threatened, I am of the view that a national organisation like the appellant, which claims to have studied and made research on the disputed project, can and should be attributed a threshold standing as having sufficient interest in the matter."[26]

There is need for a clear recognition that sustainable development must be "human-focused" or "people centered." In designing development programs and projects, together with narrowly economic

---

[25] Richard Jolly, "Adjustment with a Human Face," in *Human Development: The Neglected Dimension,* ed. Khadija Haq and Üner Kirdar (Islamabad: North-South Roundtable, 1986), 388.

[26] "Dr. Mohiuddin Farooque vs Bangladesh," *Dhaka Law Report* 49 (1997): 6.

appraisals of cost and benefit, there must be an assessment of their environmental, social, and human rights impact. How will the benefits and costs of a project or program be distributed among the different sections of a community? A sensitive assessment will need to be made of the social impact a development project or program, and not only of its environment impact. This assessment would involve taking into account such matters as: How will it affect different sections of a community, especially women and children, the poor and the vulnerable? Is it likely to favor the privileged and the powerful? Will the implementation involve procedures that would enable the more powerful to pre-empt the benefits, or lead to corruption? What impact will it have on human rights?

Guidelines have begun to be framed based on experience in different areas. For example, the World Bank has devised certain norms in the form of an operational manual pertaining to social issues associated with involuntary resettlement in projects it has financed. The bank's approach is to ensure "that the displaced persons are at least enabled to regain their previous standard of living and that they are as far as possible socially and economically integrated into the local communities. Planning and financing re-settlement should thus be an integral part of the project, since there is growing recognition that those who are relocated feel powerless and alienated when uprooted from familiar surroundings resulting in the disruption of community structures and social networks and a weakening of social cohesion."[27]

In the area of adjustment, it has been persuasively urged that "adjustment policy with a human focus will remain a sham—'an attempt to paint a smile on a face with tears'—if it is seen only as a matter of a change in the macro-economic policy of governments. Instead it must involve a move to a more people-focused process of adjustment, a more fundamental restructuring, a shift to much greater self-reliance, to decentralisation, small-scale production and community action, empowerment of people and households."[28]

An alternative to large-scale irrigation projects, which tend to benefit rich landowners who acquire the status of "water lords" based on their ownership of water pumps, has been devised by certain non-government organizations (NGOs) in Bangladesh. The project aims at enabling the landless and the rural poor to acquire and run mechanized

---

[27] B. G. Verghese, *Waters of Hope: Integrated Water Resource Development and Regional Cooperation within the Himalayan-Ganga-Brahmaputra-Barak Basin* (New Delhi: Oxford & IBH Pub. Co., 1990), 209.

[28] Jolly, "Adjustment with a Human Face," 390.

irrigation equipment. Thus, a group is formed of around twenty landless and land-poor farmers, who acquire a shallow tube-well to irrigate some six hectares of land through loans provided by the NGO. About 2400 hectares have been brought under irrigation as a result of such projects, benefiting the families of some 3600 group workers, creating employment for nearly 400, and training dozens of mechanics. The loan repayment rate has been nearly 80 percent.[29]

Similar success in the area of resource management is reported from Nepal where local community management has replaced control by state bureaucracies. Thus in the Arun Valley "by mutual agreement everyone in the village shared the right to use the forest as they needed, but no one was allowed to clear the land. To promote a sustained yield, the headmen of the village assigned certain rights to gather firewood in certain areas of each woodlot, and households jealously guard their territories.... Trivial uses of wood are discouraged.... The fundamental concept of a renewable resource is also recognised, and the headman will sometimes declare a moratorium on cutting if a certain plot shows signs of really excessive use that will soon lead to complete exhaustion."[30]

A recent United Nations Development Program (UNDP) report recommends policy measures for priority objectives. To reduce rural-urban disparities, the proportion of resources allocated to rural areas must increase, and even more important, the decisions about priorities and resource allocations should be made locally. Such decentralization of the decision making for the allocation of public goods may be one of the most important ways of reducing rural-urban gaps.

Female-male disparities have to be tackled at several levels. Laws need to be changed to provide equal access to assets and employment opportunities. The institutions that provide credit and disseminate technology need to be restructured to reach many more women. Reforms are also needed to bring about full female participation in political, bureaucratic, and economic decision making at every level. People are placed at the center of development, as the agents and beneficiaries of the development process. People's need and interests should guide the direction of development, and people should be fully involved in propelling economic growth and social progress.

There is growing awareness around the world of the integral link between sustainable development, human rights, people's participation and democracy. The African Charter for People Participation in

---

[29] Harry Bhaskara, et al., *Against All Odds—Breaking the Poverty Trap* (London: Panos, 1989), 44–62.

[30] Seddon, *Nepal*, 268.

Development and Transformation (1990) recognizes that the crisis engulfing Africa is "not only an economic crisis but also a human, legal, political, and social crisis." It acknowledges that this is the result in many instances of over-centralization of power; of impediments to effective participation in power; and of impediments to the effective participation of the overwhelming majority of the people in social, political, and economic development. The charter reaffirms that popular participation

in essence is the empowerment of the people to effectively involve themselves in creating the structures, and in designing policies and programmes that serve the interest of all as well as to effectively contribute to the development process and share equitably in its benefits. Therefore, there must be an opening up of political processes to accommodate freedom of opinions, tolerate differences, accept consensus on issues as well as ensure the effective participation of the people and their organizations and associations. This requires action on the part of all, first and foremost of the people themselves. But equally important are the actions of the State and the international community to create the necessary conditions for such an empowerment and to facilitate effective popular participation in social and economic life. This requires that the political system evolve to allow for democracy and full participation by all sections of our societies.

The Manila Declaration on People's Participation and Sustainable Development (1984) emphasizes that "sustainable human communities can be achieved only through a people centered development" and declares that:

A people-centered development seeks to return control over resources to the people and their communities, to be used in meeting their own needs. This creates incentives for the reasonable stewardship of resources that is essential to sustainability.

A people-centered development seeks to broaden political participation, building from a base of strong people's organisations and participatory local government. It seeks the opportunity for the people to obtain a secure livelihood based on the intensive, yet sustainable, use of renewable resources. It builds from the values and cultures of the people. Political and economic democracy are its cornerstone.

To promote sustainable development programs, governments, international financial institutions, and donor agencies need to be persuaded to change course and to develop strategies for the integrated implementation of human rights in conformity with the Rio Principles of Sustainable Development.

CONCLUDING OBSERVATIONS

Dom Hélder Câmara's teaching and example lead us to delve into the depths of our own humanity, a profound sense of human solidarity and compassion for every fellow human being, so that the moral and spiritual environment for the advance of civilization and the establishment of a humane world order can be achieved. It is only in that environment that justice can be promoted.

Parallel to the UN Conference in Rio (which had brought together the heads of states), members of civil society and NGOs assembled in the NGO forum. The forum provided ordinary women and men opportunity for sharing concerns and views about the damaging consequences of the development model grounded in pursuit of growth and consumption to the exclusion of human and environmental concerns. They spoke as true disciples of Dom Hélder Câmara when they judged the current thought and action that dominated economic policy to be "a path to collective self destruction not to self development." In the declaration adopted by the forum, they resolved to define their vision for an alternative future, candidly acknowledging that there were no clear models; but that a beginning towards crafting that alternative could be made by declaring their commitment to certain principles on which there was a broadly shared consensus. These included the following:

- *The fundamental purpose of economic organization is to meet the community's basic needs, such as for food, shelter, clothing, education health, and the enjoyment of culture; this purpose must take priority over all other forms of consumption, particularly wasteful and destructive forms of consumption such as consumerism and military spending.*

- *The quality of human life depends more on the development of social relationships, creativity, cultural and artistic expression, spirituality, and opportunity to be a productive member of the community than on the ever increasing consumption of material goods.*

- *It is essential to sustainability that economic life be organized around decentralized, relatively self-reliant local economies that control and manage their own productive resources, providing all people an equitable share in the control and benefits of productive resources, and giving them the right to safeguard their own environmental and social standards. Trade between such local economies, as between nations, should be just and balanced, and where the rights and interests of corporations conflict with the rights and interests of the community, the latter must prevail.*

- *All elements of society, irrespective of gender, class, or ethnic identity, have a right and obligation to participate fully in the life and decisions of the community. The presently poor and disenfranchised, in particular, must become full participants. Women's roles, needs, values, and wisdom are especially central to decision making on the fate of the earth. There is an urgent need to involve women at all levels of policy making, planning and implementation on an equal basis with men.*

- *Knowledge is humanity's one infinitely expandable resource, and beneficial knowledge in whatever form, including technology, is a part of the collective human heritage and should be freely shared with all who might benefit from it.*

- *Transparency must be the fundamental premise underlying decision making in all public institutions, including at international levels.*

Finally, the women and men who framed the declaration acknowledged that the thinking underlying its principles had been enriched by the teachings of many religious traditions represented among them. They understood the central place of spiritual values and spiritual development in the society they aimed to create. The elaboration of a normative framework for sustainable development would be a positive contribution towards protecting the interests of the poor and the powerless, and towards their liberation from poverty, which could truly claim to be inspired by Dom Hélder Câmara.

The Psalms teach us to lend our voice to all creatures:
to the mountains and the waters;
to the trees and the birds;
to the light that comes from above
and to the earth that provides for us;
to the creatures of the sea, from the tiniest fish to the whale.

Who has seen the same dawn twice?
Who has seen the same sunset twice?

It is a pity that there are people who will go through life
never having thought of watching the sunrise!
Or without thanking our dear friend at nightfall!

Ah, but would you like to have seen
the splendour of the act of creation?
Then just think, creation is made anew,
instant by instant, at God's hands.

Dom Hélder Câmara
Sister Earth

3 | *Reflections on eco-justice*

BAS WIELENGA

Hélder Câmara—passionate fighter against injustice, untiring friend of the pauper, and forceful voice for silently suffering masses all over the world—was driven by a vision of faith that centered on an all-inclusive affirmation of people's right to live life to the fullest, and yet realizing the potential given to humans by God the creator. His analysis of the causes of injustice rightly focused on local and global structures of inequality and exploitation dividing rich and poor nations and rich and poor within each nation. He shared the widespread hope of the early decades of post-war and post-independence development efforts that human creativity, aided by modern science and technology, would be able to provide for all when the structures of injustice have been overcome.

The struggles against unjust structures are more urgent today than ever before. New waves of globalization, dominated by transnational companies (TNCs) and promoted by global institutions such as World Trade Organization (WTO), International Monetary Fund (IMF), and World Bank, are inundating national economies and uprooting millions of small producers, traditional fisher folk, peasants, and artisans from their livelihoods, while depriving many others of their jobs in industry. A prophetic and priestly concern, as that of Dom Hélder Câmara, is needed to fight the fatalism that defends silent indifference and failure to confront the problems with the excuse that there is no alternative.

In many respects the parameters and the perspectives for resistance against injustice and for the transformation of society have changed dramatically to the disadvantage of the poor. Hélder Câmara and others had some hope that the United Nations Conference on Trade and Development (UNCTAD) and other UN organizations could support

Dr. Bas Wielenga has been teaching biblical theology as well as social analysis at the Tamilnadu Theological Seminary in Madurai, South India, since 1975. Earlier he was research scholar in the Christian Institute for the Study of Religion and Society in Bangalore. In the 1960s he worked in the Ecumenical Centre, Hendrik Kraemer House, in Berlin. He has published in the fields of Christian-Marxist dialogue, biblical theology, and social analysis.

structural changes toward more equal and fair relations for global trade and development. Today the WTO, dominated by the interests of global capital, has taken over and UNCTAD is being sidelined. Whatever the deficiencies of the Soviet bloc as led by the USSR, its very existence limited the scope of global capital and helped create spaces in which nonaligned countries and people's movements could make themselves heard. In those days advocates for the poor of the Third World such as Hélder Câmara could expect some sympathetic hearing in socialist and even social-democratic circles, however feeble the actual interventions by those forces might have been. The abandoning of the traditions of the moderate left, led by Tony Blair and Gerhard Schroeder, among others, has reduced the possibilities of gaining political support for struggles aimed at bringing global capital under some form of control. The "third way" of which they speak offers no alternative. It attempts to achieve economic growth along with social fairness, by seeking a path between the old welfare state and survival-of-the-fittest capitalism. But it leads straight to the altars of neo-liberalism where adherents confess their faith in free trade, global competition, and efficiency, while some rhetorical leftovers of the leftist tradition are used to put a vaguely human face on the operations of global capitalism.

But we need not lose all hope. The plight of people is such that resistance movements spring up again and again. Brazil, Hélder Câmara's home country, shows through the land occupation campaigns of the landless and through the mass appeal of the Workers Party that seeds sown in the past may yet bear fruit. For new alliances to emerge, a rethinking and reorientation has to take place. Solutions proposed thirty years ago, based on the assumption that accelerated growth could be a basis for a just redistribution of wealth, are no longer feasible. The looming eco-crises are pointing to a "second contradiction" of capital.[1] While the first contradiction is that of labor and capital, the second contradiction is between the logic of never-ending accumulation of capital and the conditions of production that put limits on what can be produced and consumed. The resources of nature are limited, and the capacity of society and of humans to cope with the logic of capital is limited. This insight has not yet penetrated deeply into circles and movements with a leftist inspiration. Those who seek to forge red-green alliances between differing political parties confront many obstacles.

The problems of dwindling resources; pollution of air, water, and land; the poisoning of the food chain; and the risks of hastily developed and introduced technologies, such as nuclear energy and genetic

---

[1] See the theoretical discussions in *Capitalism Nature Socialism: A Journal of Socialist Ecology.*

engineering, are serious enough. But the way some ecological movements have introduced them has deeply antagonized movements fighting against injustices. Demands to close polluting factories or to stop logging without concern for workers who would lose their jobs have created the suspicion that ecology is a concern of upper and middle-class people, for whom the survival of rare butterflies or monkeys is more important than the survival of workers.

This impression is fostered especially by so-called deep ecologists who criticize Jewish-Christian traditions and humanism for their anthropocentrism, which they identify as a root cause of the eco-crisis. Hélder Câmara would certainly fall under this critique. Humans are indeed central to his worldview and worldwide conscientization efforts in a double way. He identifies human selfishness as the root cause of personal and structural injustice. But he does not blame the human species as such, as certain ecologists and preachers tend to do. He points at the victims of selfishness and injustice and makes their liberation his central concern. He presupposes that selfish people can repent and that their victims can rise up and shake off the chains that enslave them.

This concern for the weakest members of the human species and the affirmation of their right to life does entail a conflict with ecological views that give priority to the survival of the human species and argue that nature lets the weaker exemplars of a species perish so they do not burden the species in its struggle for survival. Such a biologistic approach, be it Malthusian, Social-Darwinist, fascist, or a variety of "deep ecology," cannot be reconciled with the Jewish, Christian, and humanist traditions.

On the other hand, the critique of destructive potentials in modern science and technology, as presented by ecologists, is a challenge to a widespread uncritical embracing of technological progress as the solution to the problems of poverty and development. The generation of Hélder Câmara has been reluctant to acknowledge the ambiguities and destructive potentials of technological progress. When the first Indian prime minister, Jawaharlal Nehru, spoke of factories and dams as "temples of modern India" he was over-optimistic and did not realize the extent to which science and technology are part of the structures of injustice threatening human and non-human life.[2]

In the context of a reflection on education for liberation, Hélder Câmara speaks of the wonders of science and its promise. He lists "the achievements and future possibilities of industrial chemistry, the

---

[2] In January 2001, recalling Nehru's comments, another prime minister, Atal Behari Vajpayee, observed that "the new temples of modern day India are the information technology parks and campuses of software companies…"

achievements of space travel, the achievements of medicine…, the achievements of bio-chemistry in agriculture and the conquest of the depths of the sea, modern means of transport and communication and their future possibilities." He even wonders, "Will they soon be able to create life in the laboratory or abolish death?" He comments, "We should not be afraid of progress. Man has only just begun to accomplish what he was created for; he was commanded by God to subdue the earth and finish the work of creation."[3] The notion of humans as co-creators with God appears in several places and seems to function as a theological grounding for this technological optimism.

This approach is open to criticism not only from the side of ecological movements, which can point at the deadly dangers of industrial chemistry, pesticides poisoning the food chain, and terminator technology depriving peasants of control over their seeds, while risking uncontrollable effects on the environment. It also has no solid biblical basis, in spite of its reference to the commandment to subdue the earth (Gen. 1:28), which since Francis Bacon has been a standard justification for the conquest of nature.[4]

The following biblical and political reflections are meant to highlight the inner connections between the struggle for social justice and the concern for "the integrity of creation," as the ecumenical movement has called it. It should be noted that another side of Hélder Câmara affirms this close connection, in the beauty and wisdom of his contemplation of God-given life. He practiced the eco-friendly art of contemplation in the silence of the night and the noise of the day. He may have been uncritical at times about the technological creations of human co-creators with God. But his meditative mind remained open to a receptive sense of dependence on God-given creation, as when he listened to a Beduin who told him that when one star is absent a caravan may lose its way.[5]

ECO-JUSTICE AND THE QUESTION OF ANTHROPOCENTRISM

Hélder Câmara seems to confirm the fears of many ecologists. He places humans in the center and seems unaware of the life-destroying effects of the conquest of nature by human co-creators armed with the latest science and technology. The question is whether anthropocentrism is the root cause, whether eco-hostility is unavoidable when we hold that

[3] Hélder Câmara, *The Desert Is Fertile* (London: Sheed & Ward, 1974), 30.

[4] For a further discussion of ideological trends in ecological movements see Bas Wielenga, *Towards an Eco-Just Society* (Bangalore: Centre for Social Action, 1999).

[5] Hélder Câmara, *Mach aus mir einen Regenlogen: Mitternächtliche Meditationen* (Zurich, 1981), 6.

humans occupy a special place in relation to non-human nature, as the Bible undoubtedly does.

Before going into the biblical approach, it should be noted that not all ecologists see anthropocentrism as the core problem.[6] Scholars such as Ted Benton, Murray Bookchin, and Ramachandra Guha agree that the relationship between humans and nature has become alienated and destructive. They also agree that nature cannot be treated as dead matter as has been done since Bacon and Descartes. But they refuse to discuss the problem in terms of "humans" or "life" or "the earth" being in the center. It cannot be denied, they argue, that the human species plays a unique role in relation to other forms of life and to the planet as a whole. In modern capitalist society, that role has become destructive. But human society need not be as destructive as capitalist civilization is. And not all humans should be equally blamed for the havoc done to nature by capitalism. One could even say that the situation is so serious because humans are no longer in the center; capital, with its logic of unlimited accumulation, is. However alienated humans may be in industrial society, eventually they can come to their senses when they see the havoc of a destroyed forest or realize how pesticides and air pollution cause cancer. Humans can stop and turn around, but capitalism can only hurry on.

Viewed in this way Hélder Câmara's passionate critique of injustice and his appeal to the human conscience can be extended to include the critique of injustice done to nature and the appeal to break with destructive practices. At this point, the term *eco-justice* may be introduced as a means to link up both concerns.

The term *eco-justice* originated, if I am not mistaken, in the United States, where it is used to oppose discriminatory practices of waste-disposal and environmental protection at the expense of vulnerable, often racial minorities. The pattern can be seen all around the world: the poor are forced to live in the most polluted places, under the most unhealthy conditions. In general, it can be said that they are most affected by the eco-crisis. This is true for Blacks and Native Americans in the US, as well as for Dalits and displaced Adivasis in India. Moreover, ecologically irresponsible practices discriminate against future generations, which are deprived of their share of resources, and against non-human co-species, which are denied fair living space. It follows that the term *eco-justice* may be used in the wider sense of doing justice to the relationships among humans as well as between humans and non-human nature.

---

[6] See Wielenga, *Towards an Eco-Just Society*, 135ff.

The concept of eco-justice appears to me particularly appropriate and useful if applied to the biblical approach and its alleged anthropocentrism. Obviously, in the Bible humans are assigned a special and important, even a central role. But this role is shaped and controlled by a triangular framework of relationships which is so basic that it can be stated that the biblical view of reality is neither anthropocentric nor eco- or geocentric, nor even theocentric, but covenant-centered. The Bible understands reality as a complex set or web of relationships of a covenant character. And it understands history as the process in which the God-given flow of life through the channels of these relationships is becoming blocked by egocentrism. Because the role of humans is central, it needs liberating interventions to remove the barriers of injustice and accumulation so that life can flow again through sharing in solidarity, based on God's covenant with the earth and all life and with God's people Israel and the poor.

Of course, the Bible does not reflect on ecological questions in present-day terms. Its outlook reflects concerns that arose within a traditional subsistence economy in a developing class society and in confrontation with conquering empires. Within those contexts, the relevant relationships are articulated. The biblical terminology of justice, *tsedaqah,* can be employed to express the demand to do the right thing, to do justice to the covenant relationships, and to act according to what the sustenance of those relationships requires.

Usually it is assumed that the biblical focus on the relationship of God and humans tends to ignore the importance of non-human nature. It is also true for other religious traditions that special attention is given to the questions of how humans are provided with food and other resources. And nobody should consider the question of "our daily bread" as an irrelevant concern. But the Bible also affirms and refers to non-human nature beyond human control, and independent of human needs. It reminds humans that they are not the only ones who matter and that not everything revolves around them. It points at a wide range of reality beyond their control, a reality created and sustained by God the creator. While Psalm 8, following Genesis 1, emphasizes human dominion over beasts and birds and fish (having primarily domestic animals such as sheep and oxen in mind), Psalm 104 sings of realms of nature not under human control or designed to serve human needs. They are in direct relationship to God who gives food to the lions and plays with Leviathan in the sea. That is all part of the flow of life that is sustained by the Spirit of God (Ps. 104:27–30). The meaning of that reality and the rationale for its existence cannot be expressed in terms of its utility for humans.

Out of the whirlwind, Job hears God's stern message not to think in his suffering that he is the center of the cosmos and in the know about everything (Job 38–39). Does he know the way to the place of light and darkness? Does he control the clouds or the calving of the hinds? God has let the wild ass go free, "to which I have given the steppe for its home."[7] Not all animals are meant to be domesticated: "Is the wild ox willing to serve you? Will it spend the night at your crib?"[8] "Is it at your command that the eagle mounts up and makes its nest on high?"[9] This accumulation of questions builds a strong case against an anthropocentric worldview. The presupposition is that non-human creation has its own spaces and its own right of existence, independent of its utility for humans. Martin Buber sees in this the justice of the creator at work who gives "to all His creatures His boundary, so that each may become fully itself."[10]

The book of Job also includes a powerful poem that expresses admiration for the capacity of humans to dig up the earth in the search for silver, gold, iron, and copper (Job 28). Such mining is beyond the falcon's eye and the lion's path (Job 28:7–8). Miners "put their hand to the flinty rock, and overturn mountains by the roots" (28:9). But before technological optimism and fascination can consolidate their hold over our minds, a sobering, penetrating question interrupts the lyrical enthusiasm about mining: "But where shall wisdom be found? Mortals do not know the way to it, and it is not found in the land of the living" (28:12–13).

The Bible does not oppose the development of human knowledge and technological reach. Prometheus need not steal the fire from heaven, because human empowerment is part of the creation story. The Bible displays deep awareness both that humans are able to do amazing things, as Hélder Câmara loved to affirm, and that danger inheres in their hubris and greed for power. There is the problem of humans trying to occupy center stage, building towers of Babel, and upsetting the balances. Human violence undermines relationships and eventually triggers eco-catastrophes, as is paradigmatically told in the story of the flood. Wisdom that respects the limitations of life is needed in order to do justice to the life-sustaining relationships between *Adam* and *adamah* (the ground), humans and non-human creation, present and future

---

[7] Job 39:6.

[8] Job 39:9.

[9] Job 39:27.

[10] Martin Buber, "A God Who Hides His Face," in *The Dimensions of Job*, ed. Nahum N. Glatzer (New York: Schocken Bks., Inc., 1969), 63.

generations; and the relationship of all together with the giver of life, God the creator.

Wisdom consists of fearing and respecting God the creator, and departing from evil (Job 28:28). Prophetic texts presuppose the same intricate interdependency. The lack of "knowledge of God in the land," the breaking of all bounds, and murder following murder (Hos. 4:1–2) have ecological consequences in the vision of Hosea:

> *Therefore the land mourns,*
> *and all who live in it languish,*
> *together with the wild animals*
> *and the birds of the air;*
> *and even the fish of the sea are perishing. (Hos. 4:3)*

A late text in the book of Isaiah directly relates such breakdowns to the breaking of the covenant God made with Noah:

> *The earth dries up and withers,*
> *the world languishes and withers;*
> *the heavens languish together with the earth.*
> *The earth lies polluted*
> *under its inhabitants;*
> *for they have transgressed laws,*
> *violated the statutes,*
> *broken the everlasting covenant. (Isa. 24:4–5)*

The chapter speaks of the encompassing breakdown, the chaos that follows, the lack of wine and the end of the joys of life.

Having in mind both this apocalyptic text and the warnings of ecologists today, we wonder how life in its fullness can be affirmed. And simultaneously we explore how the drift toward destruction caused by the breaking of all bounds can be resisted.

ABUNDANCE OF LIFE OR ACCUMULATION

One basic notion on which the life-sustaining covenant relationships among God-land-people or God-earth-humankind are based is the conviction that life is a gift. Life is given, land is given, rain is given, and food is given by a God who cares. And when not only green plants but also animals are "given" for food, the commandment is added not to eat flesh with its blood, because blood represents life (Gen. 9:3f; cf. Lev. 17:12, Deut. 12:23, Acts 15:20). Moreover, as later laws specify, only certain species of clean animals are given for food, namely animals that do not themselves take life. They remind us that we depend on life given to us. That is why the same innocent, life-giving animals, rather than life-taking animals, are chosen for sacrifice in worship. We may not all become vegetarians, but we are all expected to honor and respect life and to care for it as a precious gift.

This given life is meant to multiply, to blossom in all its diversity and interconnectedness. God's blessing is seen in procreation, in the bearing of fruits, and in the abundance of life. The commandment of the creator, "Be fruitful and multiply" (Gen. 1:28 and 9:1), may sound problematic today in view of rapid population growth. These texts were written in a time when underpopulation rather than overpopulation could cause problems, and when households needed more hands in order to survive. Today humanity's urgent need is not for an increase in the population but for an increase in the quality of life for all people on the planet. How can we share space and resources in a way that allows all to live a full life in dignity? Taking justice in the sharing of resources as our aim, we find that the basic problem is not population growth (as Hélder Câmara rightly pointed out) or scarcity (as the economic textbooks want us to believe). Instead the basic problem is the way a minority of rich countries, and the upper classes in all countries, have appropriated and accumulated the God-given resources of the earth, and used violence to deny others access to these resources. It is their expansionism and wasteful devouring of resources that is burdening the planet and causing scarcity, even of fresh air and clean water.

Multiplication of life depends on the biblical vision of the sustaining Spirit of God breathing the breath of life, and on the gift of rain in its seasons, and on human work. That is the supplementing point of the older creation narrative of Genesis 2, which speaks of the rain and the work—literally *service*—of the humans in tilling the ground. *Adam* (humankind) and *adamah* (ground) belong together. Here we find the co-creators of whom Hélder Câmara was fond of speaking. Different aspects of technological humanism have to be considered. Hélder Câmara focuses on the creativity of human work, Adam Smith on its productivity if properly divided and managed, and Karl Marx on its role as the source of surplus value and thus of profit based on exploitation. Ecologists focus on the impact all this creativity, productivity, and exploitation makes on nature. In human work the social, the economic, and the ecological are intertwined.

In the book of Deuteronomy, which affirms the blessing of life in its abundance, we can discern a cyclic sequence. It starts from God's blessings and gifts; it passes through human work, and through the sharing of the fruits of labor, which is seen as the condition for the cycle to continue, as God blesses the work of human hands which then results in increased prosperity[11] and well-being. The crucial point is what is being done with the fruits: Are they shared, or are they appropriated and accumulated at the expense of others? Justice is the condition for the continuation of the flow of life. The expression "that the LORD your God may bless you in all the work that you undertake" occurs at the conclusion of major reform proposals such as tithing for the poor, release of debt-slaves, prohibition of interest, among others.[12] This vision sees humans as blessed cooperators with God in their work, as long as they are guided by the demands of justice as we find them in the Torah. Social justice—sharing the fruits with the poor according to legislation to protect their right to life and not accumulation—leads in this vision to prosperity.

Of course, we cannot directly apply the reform proposals of Deuteronomy. But we need to listen to its basic vision, which focuses on God's blessing not as the result of labor and its exploitation, but as the source of an economy liberated from the never-ending enslaving and excluding law of accumulation. As Frank Cruesemann translates for our present-day context, this would mean that we search for ways to use accumulated wealth not principally for further accumulation, but for creating conditions that enable all human beings to do useful work. Technological developments will reduce the number of people who can find employment in mass production. But the work of caring for young and old, for sick and handicapped; the work of education and formation; the work of care for the environment by planting trees, conserving soil for the next generation; and—last but not least—the work of non-destructive agriculture can employ all human beings who now are unjustly denied the right to work by the logic of accumulation. One basic demand of justice would be fulfilled in that way. This vision also points to the need to rethink the character of work. In industrial society, the focus has been on production. The work of care is undervalued, and yet in that work there is a close affinity to the work of God to whose care we owe our life.

The call, the imperative invitation to be fruitful and multiply and to fill the earth (Gen. 1:28 and 9:1), presupposes that God's blessing goes beyond austere subsistence. Something of God's glory is seen in the blossoming of nature, the sprouting and multiplication of life (Genesis 1, Psalm 104). The problem is that abundance or surplus attracts greed for

---

[11] See Frank Cruesemann, "Gottes Fürsorge und Menschliche Arbeit: Ökonomie und Soziale Gerechtigkeit in Biblischer Sicht," in *Eigentum: Freiheit und Fluch: Ökonomische und biblische Einwürfe,* ed. Rainer Kessler u. Eva Loos (Gütersloh: Kaiser, 2000), 43ff.

[12] See Deut. 14:28–29; 15:18; 23:20f; 15:10; 16:15; 24:13; 24:19.

accumulation, whereas it is meant for sharing. The good shepherd of John 10 wants his sheep to have life in abundance, but he even has to lay down his life because of thieves who come to steal and kill.

The multiplication of life and the bounty of nature have built-in limits. Animals stop killing when their hunger is stilled. Ants and other creatures may be clever in storing food for one or two seasons. But neither food nor cattle nor other material possessions can be hoarded endlessly and in unlimited quantity. It is money, an artifact distinguishing humans from animals, that makes limitless accumulation possible. The discovery that surplus can be sold, and that the means of payment, gold or silver, can be hoarded, has turned the abundance of nature into a source of accumulated wealth and power which sooner or later turns against people and the environment.

Of course, gold and silver can be used in different ways and even they can be seen as a result of God's blessing. These metals may serve to beautify the temple or to invest in irrigation works or to be shared with the poor. But they have a tremendously dangerous capacity to place themselves in the center and to destroy the elementary relationship between God and humans, among fellow humans, and with the earth. They tend to turn into an idol, Mammon or Moloch, demanding the sacrifice of life not for the sake of life, but for the sake of profit, the accumulation of "dead labor," as Marx saw it. In such sacrifice of life, the pursuit of wealth may lead to devastating wars. Its accumulation may demand and exploit slave labor, degrading human beings. Isaiah 2:7–9 makes this connection, and places it in striking contrast to the preceding vision of peace in Isa. 2:1–5.

> Their land is filled with silver and gold,
> and there is no end to their treasures;
> their land is filled with horses,
> and there is no end to their chariots.
> Their land is filled with idols;
> they bow down to the work of their hands,
> to what their own fingers have made.
> And so people are humbled,
> and everyone is brought low.

The ambiguous relationship between the abundance of life and the life-threatening accumulation based on it is reflected in the biblical usage of the word "treasury" and "storehouse." The word *otsar* is used for the treasury of heaven from which God the creator gives rain and wind in order "to bless all your undertakings" (Deut. 28:12; cf., Jer. 10:12–13, Ps. 33:7; cf. Matt. 5:45). Combined with human labor, this gift results in the fruits of the earth. The same word, however, is used for the treasury of gold and silver which the rulers and the rich accumulate. These treasures, heaped up in temple and palace, do not provide security and do not foster life because they are the target of conquerors again and again, as the books of Kings narrate (1 Kings 7:51, et al.). These conquerors in the Bible are depicted as those who forget that political and economic life is embedded in God's creation, and that life continues to be dependent on giving and sharing. God announces judgment on Pharaoh, who in his hubris says, "My Nile is my own, I made it for myself" (Ezek. 29:3).

Today transnational companies may claim as their own the resources of the forest, of the earth, of the oceans, and of the genes, saying "I have the patents even on the basic forms of life." Against such arrogant appropriation of what are God's gifts to all we find the pronouncement of judgment throughout the Bible. What has exalted itself will be brought low. Creation, which is affected by this wrongful appropriation, plays a role in judgment. In Ezekiel the chaos-making power, the dragon-like Pharaoh, lies in his streams. He will be caught with a hook and cast into the wilderness, and given as food "to the beasts of the earth and to the birds of the air" (29:5). He can no longer "trouble the waters" and "foul the rivers" (32:2). Chapter 31 carries the same message, using the mythical image of a mighty cosmic tree which gives life, shade, and food to all creatures as in the garden of God. But when the empire starts to think of itself as that all-embracing cosmic tree, it has become an overpowering product of pride and has to be cut down.

JUSTICE ALLIANCES FOR LIFE'S SAKE

Ezekiel envisages that such accumulators of power and wealth will be caught in the divine dragnet and discarded. They do not have the last word. But sometimes, as in the book of Job, people feel overwhelmed by the experience of powerlessness over against the forces of chaos which the "great dragon" represents.[13] As noted above, Ezekiel 38–39 speaks of the relative autonomy of the various eco-realms of creation, but the next two chapters address the problem of the destructive powers of Leviathan and Behemoth. These are not just a crocodile and hippopotamus, as some commentators assume who read these chapters as a further demonstration of the awesome glory of God's creation.[14] They are indeed part of creation (see 40:15–19); but they are also political animals who have appropriated creation, and represent death-dealing imperial forces.

---

[13] Bas Wielenga, "Facing Monsters of Chaos," *COELI* 84 (winter 1997–98): 2–11.

[14] I follow here the interpretation of Jürgen Ebach, *Leviathan und Behemoth: Eine biblische Erinnerung wider die Kolonisierung der Lebenswelt durch das Prinzip der Zweckrationalität* (Paderborn: F. Schöningh, 1984).

And Job, mirroring post-exilic and powerless suffering Israel, has to admit that he cannot draw them out with a fishhook, which is precisely what God has promised to do in Ezekiel (cf. Ezek. 29:4, Job 41:1). The text does not assure directly that God will act once again as liberator, but the whirlwind from which God speaks may well be the storm of his judgment. It indicates that the pharaohs of the days of post-exilic Israel, as well as today's triumphant global capitalists, might have to face plagues that confront them with the consequences of their irresponsible behavior. Will a new exodus path open through the sea and the desert? Will the kings of pride (Job 41:34) hit the limits, and will the fate of Job turn and the flow of blessing return to him? Whatever liberating turns we dare hope for, we have to address the question: What can be done now? How can we prepare for a people's exodus from the pharaohs of today?

Whoever says "nothing can be done," or "there is no alternative," contributes to the power of global capital over the minds of people and to the closure of any future. Instead, we may learn from Hélder Câmara to intervene on various levels, through challenging protests, organized resistance, lived alternatives, nurturing hope, and widening small openings. A great variety of people movements show that people still fight back, still hope. How then can Christians forget that those who hunger and thirst for justice are called blessed?

In June 2000, in Hofgeismar, Germany, 150 participants in an international conference on Faith, Economy, and Theology discussed the theme "Faith Communities and Social Movements Facing Globalization." We discussed the contrast between the political economy of death and the political economy of life. The first treats nature as a warehouse of human, natural, and genetic resources, as raw materials to be used in industrial production aimed at profits, but at the cost of depletion, pollution, and deadly risks. The second centers on life, first of all, through a subsistence economy of food and health, and supplemented by trading goods and services in the exchange economy, all of which are within the limits given in creation as the foundation and context of all life. What is needed is to find ways to convert the present global system to a viable people's economy of life. A few tentative points may be made:

Drawing strength from local roots

Câmara was a globetrotter for justice. But his worldwide appeal drew strength from his local involvement in North-East Brazil. It was from his Galilee of impoverished peasants and fisher folk that he took to the roads to confront the mighty in seeking justice. He came from there when he visited the powerful in their metropolitan centers. Such rootedness and orientation from the perspective of the marginalized remains vital today. Global networks need strong local roots. I offer two examples from India. Local artisans, fish workers along the coasts of India, have built up their local organization through years of struggle against destructive trawling and deep-sea high-tech fishing, and on that basis were able to make an amazing international contribution. They have brought together fish workers from many countries through what is now called World Forum of Fish Workers. Second, indigenous people and other poor peasants in the Narmada valley in Central India have been struggling for more than fifteen years against destructive giant dams. It is on that basis of sustained local struggles that they have been able to link up with other organizations inside the country and worldwide.

Such protest movements have started the difficult work of building alliances without dominant vanguards. In India, for example, the National Alliance of Peoples Movements brings together, for mutual support, organizations of peasants, fish workers, workers, Dalits, and women. They address a broad agenda of human rights, workers' rights, women's rights, social justice, and ecological sustainability in an overall perspective of alternative development. Elsewhere similar strategic alliances emerge, combining mass mobilization for protest with involvement in the development of constructive alternatives in agriculture, health, education, water management, housing, etc.

Resisting destructive global institutions and policies
As noted, Hélder Câmara expected some reorientation and improvement through United Nations bodies such as UNCTAD. Since that time, the rich countries, led by the USA and geared to the interests of the TNCs, have shifted global decision-making from the UN to the IMF, World Bank, and WTO. These organizations try to make the world freely accessible and safe for capital. For people, this shift means loss of livelihood and repression of human rights and of the right to protest. Movements of different backgrounds are realizing the threat, and are starting to focus their protest on WTO and IMF, as intervention in Seattle in December 1999 showed. This development has to be understood as a potentially international liberating protest from below against the latest form of imperialism, a despotic globalization from above.

Forming covenant alliances against bio-piracy
Ownership, owners' absolute freedom to choose what to do with their property, is the basis of capitalist economy, the root cause of its injustice, and the core issue in struggles for justice. Classical Marxist theory has shown how the appropriation of capital is based on the expropriation of

the mass of producers, turning them into non-owning sellers of labor-power. Capitalist development is the story of the concentration of the means of production of land, tools, and resources in the hands of some at the expense of others. This process is assuming additional dimensions today. Pesticide-producing TNCs are transfiguring themselves into "life-science" companies, buying up seed companies and claiming patent rights over seeds that have been the common property of local communities for many centuries. The enclosure of the commons at the outset of the capitalist era is now followed by the expropriation of traditional knowledge systems preserved and developed by women, tribal communities, and peasant cultures, and their appropriation by a few giant companies for the sake of the accumulation of profit. The peoples movements in India and elsewhere rightly speak of "gene-robbery" and "bio-piracy." The wealth of bio-diversity in Third World countries is being plundered, and profitable but ecologically damaging mono-crops of a few hybrid varieties are being pushed instead.

The same forces are moving to claim patent (i.e., ownership) rights over life forms, including parts of the human body. Earlier generations of workers were turned into appendages of machines. Now human genes are being mapped and brought under private control. Bio-genetics is being advertised as a triumph of science, with a promise of abundance of food and everlasting health. In spite of Hélder Câmara's optimistic expectations regarding new discoveries in the labs, we must take seriously the warnings of critical scientists and eco-movements. There is a new dimension of risk and danger to life involved. Faulty parts in cars or planes can be detected and replaced, but genetically manipulated organisms cannot be called back after they have entered the environment, the fields, and the food chain.

Life needs time and space to grow. The injustice caused by uncontrolled and unlimited accumulation in private hands denies space and time to people. It was Jeremiah's hope that people would return from exile, and that the life of people and of animals would be rooted again in the land, and that the land would be sown to bear fruit in the life-sustaining spirit of renewed covenant (Jer. 31:27, 31). The peoples movements are allying to struggle for such a reorientation in the hope that it is still possible to avoid the outcome of present policies, when "the harvest will flee away in a day of grief and incurable pain" (Isa. 17:11).

Defending democratic spaces

Protest movements need to receive political support of parties, administrators, and governments to move toward at least reduction, if not prevention of damage through minimum controls over big capital.

The abandoning of the nation state and its responsibilities plays into the hands of global capital. In any case, the movements need to defend political democracy, which allows them to organize and to gather and spread information. In a country such as India, signs point to the danger of possible fascist tendencies and developments, as state power is being used to smash the people's organizations and protests while appealing to certain identities in the pursuit of divide-and-rule policies. International solidarity is again needed in these struggles.

Work in the church

Hélder Câmara appealed to the church to live up to the potential of its faith. Even in the church, many hopes have withered since those days of the Vatican Council and a vibrant ecumenical movement. Yet the church still has many resources to wake us up, to sustain disciples and followers of Jesus: the Torah's basic call to "choose life," the Prophets' critiques of injustice and visions of hope, the praise and longing of the Psalms, the down-to-earth counsel of Wisdom, the inspiration of the Gospels: To the power of these Hélder Câmara was a convincing witness.

We are all convinced
that all human beings
are children of the same heavenly Father.
Those who have the same father are brothers and sisters;
let us treat one another as brothers and sisters.

Dom Hélder Câmara
"Providence Has Taken Me by the Hand"

Sharing hope does not mean sharing faith.
Those who do not believe have one thing in common
with those who believe—
namely, that the Lord believes in them.
Of course they can, and should, work together!

Dom Hélder Câmara
Questions for Living

4 | *A global confrontation or local conflicts?*

Many conflicts are depicted as religious wars, and as manifestations of ancestral hatred. This is most often true when such conflicts involve Christians and Muslims in the Balkans, Caucasus, Indonesia, Nigeria, and Sudan. Religious intolerance, which is more particularly associated with Islam and indiscriminately attributed to Muslims, is likely to be invoked as a determinant in such conflicts. With more or less religious and historical overtones, reference is frequently made to jihad and crusade. Expressions of what is said to be an Islamic threat instantly capture the media's attention. Perceptions of Muslims, and conflicts they are a party to, are marked to varying degrees by sensationalism, essentialism, and culturalism.

In profiling what is sensational, certain images and stories not only oversimplify complex realities, but tend to blur the picture they claim to make clear. Be they historically specific, or culturally, politically, and religiously diverse, the situations of Muslims in relation to non-Muslims are viewed by many as essentially the same. Recognizing plurality, avoiding precipitate comparisons, and refraining from amalgamation can be seen as magnification of details and failure or unwillingness to acknowledge major trends in today's world. At best, the search for intellectual rectitude and subtlety is dismissed as luxury. For their part, advocates of secular or Christian cultural supremacy and liberal proponents of respect for other cultures (sometimes idealized or made

Tarek Mitri was born in Lebanon and he is affiliated with the Greek Orthodox Patriarchate of Antioch and all the East. He now resides in Geneva, Switzerland, where he is the coordinator of Interreligious Relations and Dialogue, World Council of Churches. He is also a professor of modern history and sociology of Eastern Christianity and Christian-Muslim relations, University of Balamand, Lebanon. Dr. Mitri also serves as an occasional visiting lecturer in various universities and theological institutes in Europe. He has published books and articles on Christian-Muslim relations, interreligious dialogue, Christianity in the Arab world, Christian thought and Islam. He studied chemistry and philosophy at the American University of Beirut, and has a doctorate in social sciences from the University of Paris.

exotic) emphasize the distinctiveness of what is labeled as Islamic culture. However, their exaggerated emphasis on the status of culture and its role in explaining personal and collective behavior is less visible when they reflect on their own situations.

Religious and secular people who are involved in or affected by conflicts sometimes overstate the religious dimension of these conflicts. In the eyes of many, in the early phase of the second Palestinian uprising, the religious dispute over holy places in Jerusalem overshadowed the dispossession and humiliation of Palestinians. The various calls to jihad in Indonesia blurred the perception of many other causes of intercommunal tensions. The more a religious factor is singled out as decisive in provoking and sustaining conflicts, the stronger becomes its impact on the course of these conflicts.

Interpreting local tensions and disputes as local manifestations of a global confrontation feeds a transnational discourse on bloody borders between Christianity and Islam, or between the Muslim world and the Western world. This discourse is significantly accelerated by the diaspora of the communities and nations concerned, and it is espoused by religious organizations and, in certain cases, by policymakers in a number of countries.

In its turn, this discourse is often a factor of aggravation in local conflicts: myths, once propounded, gain a force of their own. The vulnerability of religious minorities seen to be on the wrong side of such presumed borders is accentuated. This situation is not redressed by the frequently counterproductive demand for and claim of foreign protection and by the unrealistic call for reciprocity in the treatment of threatened minorities.

In short, misinterpreting or exaggerating the role of religion in international and even intranational relations marks perceptions of local conflicts, and leads to their aggravation and to subsequent failure in addressing them. These conflicts are shaped by the propagation of a globalist discourse and its corollaries. Both factors—overemphasizing religious aspects of conflict, and viewing local conflicts as manifestations of global confrontation—are closely associated with the rift of many nations, the legitimacy crisis of a significant number of national projects, and the inadequacies of systems or practices of political participation in most religiously and ethnically plural societies such as Indonesia, Lebanon, Nigeria, or Sudan.

THE BANNER OF RELIGION

Until the late 1970s, secularization was almost universally seen as irreversible. For many years, observers tended to propose a chronological scheme for the erosion of religion. Secularization was supposed to be its ultimate phase. Conceived as a social-historical process of achieving an ever-greater autonomy of society and human thought in relation to religious institutions, symbols, and approaches to reality, secularization was equated with modernization and progress and considered inevitable. While experts recognized that many societies did not seem to follow the universal path, the divergence was perceived as an expression of delay, reflecting inadequate modernization, or as a form of provisional retrogression illustrating a last cultural resistance before the inescapable surrender.

In communist countries, eradication of religion was thought to be under way, despite some hurdles that caused delay. Problems of nationalities whose religious identity could not be ignored were addressed with deportations and population transfers in a few cases, and by granting a limited cultural and political autonomy in others.

Throughout the world, conflicts were perceived to be determined largely by economic interests, social contradictions, and political rivalries. Religion had little or no visible role in international relations. Its role in national politics was seen to be declining. Theological and political polarization within a religious community, Christian or Muslim, overshadowed the historical divisions among religions. Majorities and minorities, when mentioned, were perceived in terms of power relations and not in terms of numerical importance or cultural specifics. National integration was a prevailing model. Privatization of religion, through the combined effects of modernization and urbanization, on one hand, and through state-led nation building on a nonreligious or secular basis, on the other hand, seemed to limit the impact of religious plurality on political structures. With few exceptions, power sharing was hardly an intercommunal and interreligious issue.

Traditional religious identities were said to be waning. A significant faction of religious people and organizations made great efforts to conform to modernity tied with an irreversible secularization. Religious institutions seemed to have lost much of their influence. In this context, within Christianity and Islam, ways of transmitting religious messages underwent radical change, and transformation of content and emphasis occurred. When sociologists extrapolated the waning of religion, a number of western Christian theologians pronounced the death of the traditional discourse about God. This was their way of drawing the theological consequence of the process of secularization. One aspect of a certain liberation theology presented itself, and was understood as an attempt to rescue core revolutionary values of faith against the eroding credibility of traditional religion.[1]

A number of authors, mostly agnostic, are now repeatedly predicting a religious century to come. Some are puzzled at the prevailing expectation of a world of more mysticism, and others are preoccupied with the "the return of history," fearing wars under the banner of religion. Nevertheless, it has become clear that the prognosticators of a technological and modernizing pace who would expel religion out to the margins were wrong. They acknowledged that faith might well survive as a valued heritage in some ethnic enclaves or family customs but insisted that religion's days as a shaper of culture and history were over. Instead, religions that some theologians and other intellectuals thought had been stunted by consumer materialism or suppressed by despotic regimes have regained vigor.

It is true that religious beliefs and practices, wherever they survived, were visibly privatized in many societies. Collective identities associated with faith traditions seemed to find their expressions in a national-cultural self-understanding that, at best, integrated elements of religious memory. But the return *of* religion or the return *to* religion showed that the driving force of things metaphysical has not been consummated or extinguished, and it was the power of sentiments that bind people together in one faith. This movement took many people by surprise. It was not characterized in a clear manner or even given a precise and widely accepted name. Observers speak indiscriminately and interchangeably of the reemergence of fundamentalism, the resurgence of religion, and of its awakening or revival. Manifestations of religious self-assertion, in the particularity of their context or the distinctiveness of their faith tradition, are increasingly seen as variations of a universal phenomenon.

Needless to say, renewed interest in religion reflects two opposing and in many instances ambivalent attitudes. The first reveals satisfaction in seeing religion filling a spiritual vacuum and offering meaning and hope to a world threatened by meaninglessness, nihilism, and despair. But the second mirrors fear of the eruption of dreams and other things irrational, and anxiety about facing dangerous currents of bigotry and fanaticism.

Today the assumption that we live in a secularized and secularizing world does not meet with universal approval. A leading sociologist of

---

[1] Quite elaborate and vocal among Christians, and less so among Muslims, liberation theology was meant to draw nearer to each other the progressive forces within all religions and among people of no religion.

religion does not hesitate to affirm that in present times the world, with some exceptions, is as furiously religious as ever and in some places more so than ever.[2] To be sure, modernization has had some secularizing effects, more in some places than others. But it has also provoked powerful movements of countersecularization. Certain religious institutions have lost power in many societies, but old and new religious beliefs and practices find expression, sometimes in an explosive manner. Conversely, religiously identified institutions play social and political roles even when fewer people believe or practice the religion that these institutions represent. In extreme cases, people fight in the name of religions in which they have ceased to believe. There are conflicts between communities that have a religious past but whose religious content is irrelevant. Religions in which people have little faith continue to define communities in which people have much faith.

It is therefore essential, when assessing the role of religion in politics, be it international or national, to distinguish between political movements that may be genuinely inspired by religion and those that use religion as a convenient legitimation for political agendas based on nonreligious interests. In Egypt or Sudan, a large segment of those who advocate the implementation of shari'ah (Islamic law) may truly believe in the religious motives they avow. But we have reason to doubt that the parties involved in the Bosnian or Lebanese conflicts were really inspired by religious ideas. Marked by Ottoman heritage, conflicting relations between Christians and Muslims, *mutatis mutandis,* have revealed the precariousness of power-sharing among communities embedded in their modern political system.

The distinction between religious motivation and political interests does not imply their radical separation. In many situations, they cannot be disentangled. Somehow singularly, the Taliban rule in Afghanistan, perpetrating an intra-Muslim conflict, obeyed two divergent logics. On one hand, they claimed an Islamic universalism, emphasized the dimension of *ummah* (community), and did not hesitate, in the name of shari'ah, to oppose traditional tribal structures and culture. While they fiercely subordinated women, they condemned customary law that deprives women from inheritance and insisted on women's rights enshrined in the Qur'anic text. On the other hand, they had an ethnic base, the Pashtuns, and their conquest of power was, in a way, a return of their ethnic group to its two-centuries-old dominance. The

---

[2] See Peter L. Berger, "The Desecularization of the World: A Global Overview," in *The Desecularization of the World: Resurgent Religion and World Politics*, ed. Peter L. Berger (Washington D.C.: Ethics and Public Policy Center; Grand Rapids: Eerdmans, 1999), 1–18.

consolidation of their rule in the areas they controlled led them, with an inexorable logic, to a form of ethnic cleansing.

It is not less important when referring to tensions and conflicts involving Christians and Muslims to assume that religious revival, Islamic or otherwise, is a universal phenomenon which, to the extent it is politicized, puts at peril coexistence between communities. While some religious movements foster war, others see themselves as agents of peace in societies where the main actors in conflicts are motivated by ethnic and ethno-nationalist interests. For instance, those who manifest a stronger religious commitment, in countries such as Chechnya and Nigeria, seem to position themselves on the moderate range of the political spectrum. The official religious leaders and spiritual Sufi figures in Chechnya were able, at times, to distance themselves from the politics of nationalist leaders and warlords. In Nigeria, many religiously motivated advocates of shari'ah do not necessarily share the militancy of those whose primary aim in invoking shari'ah lies in their assertion of Hausa power.

GLOBALIZING VIEWS

It is has become difficult to discard the resonating effects in many parts of the world of a discourse on the global confrontation between Christianity or the West, and Islam. Although the contemporary Western world has largely defined itself as secular, and Muslims have gradually perceived it as such, a mounting tendency to emphasize its historical and cultural identity and portray it as Christian or Judeo-Christian does not go unnoticed. Nonwestern Christians are often identified culturally with the West, and, in the event of cultural and religious difference, suspected of political allegiance to North American and European powers even if they do not enjoy or expect any support from the West. It matters significantly less than it did a few decades ago that many Christians were major actors in anticolonial independence movements, and continue to be strong critics of western dominance.

In the Muslim world, ideological thought patterns represent the West as selfish, materialistic, and dominating. In the West the equivalent thought patterns perceive Islam as irrational, fanatical, and expansionist. In an age of global communication and migration, these thought patterns, in their subtle and not-so-subtle expressions, foster antagonism.

It is true that the issue of Islam and the West is more complex and more contingent on contemporary concerns than either proponents or opponents of cultural politics would imply. Many of the problems, such as foreign hegemony and intervention, terrorism and international threats, are confused and exaggerated. But they have become real issues, although they in the main relate to power of states, the treatment of migrant and minority groups, and the balance of forces within many developing societies.[3]

But it is not less true that the end of worldwide ideological confrontations and the globalization of Islam[4] have favored the reemergence of perceptions in which Islam and the West exist as subjective imaginary constructs influencing the way each sees the other.

In the post–Cold War world, flags seem to count tremendously, as do other symbols of cultural and religious identity. It is predicted that marching under flags leads to war. For "people seeking identity and reinventing ethnicity, enemies are essential, and the potentially most dangerous enmities occur across the fault lines between the world's major civilizations."[5]

The world has entered an era of cultural struggle in which wars and confrontations are no longer the result of clashes between individual nations or states. The clash between "the West and the rest," we are told, is religious to the extent that religions shape civilizations and they do so significantly. It is political as long as politics is determined by civilizing affinities instead of ideological options. The explosive force of such ideas lies in the projection of old hostilities between East and West on present day collective consciousness, potentially with consequences for world politics.

A significant number of Muslims see the wars in Palestine and Bosnia, to mention only two examples, as a continuation of the crusades. What was until the nineteenth century widely referred to as the Frankish invasions has come to connote global and transhistorical religious and political conquest. Western soldiers engaged in military operations against Iraq are crusaders, and so are Christian missionaries. This dehistoricizing and amalgamating process enforces the religious overtones of what for a long time had been but a major political and military confrontation in the history of western expansion. The 1991 Persian Gulf war was seen by many as a revival of the crusades, despite the fact that many Islamic states joined the US–led western military alliance. Western predominance in the Arab world, colonial and postcolonial, nurtured a view of the crusades in which Muslims see themselves retrospectively as victims, despite their position of strength

---

[3] Fred Halliday, *Islam and the Myth of Confrontation* (London: I. B. Tauris, 1996), 127.

[4] See Yvonne Haddad, "The Globalisation of Islam: The Return of the Muslims to the West," in *The Oxford History of Islam*, ed. John Esposito (Oxford: Oxford Univ. Pr., 1999).

[5] Samuel P. Huntington, *The Clash of Civilizations and the Remaking of World Order* (London: Simon and Schuster, 1997), 20.

at the time. The serenity and fortitude that characterized Muslims' reactions to the Medieval crusaders is reinterpreted in terms of the military, political, and economic subordination of the Islamic world today.

These images have been an important factor in conflicts since 1991. Soon after the Gulf war, the majority in the West became fearful of the growth of Islam on the southern shores of the Mediterranean. Many decision-takers and opinion-makers were prepared to turn a blind eye to the severe blow to democracy inflicted by the Algerian military, which led to a cruel civil war. Public images of Muslims as violent fanatics revealed a dangerous congruence for many, secular and mainstream, of the left or right, ideas that resulted in ultranationalist and xenophobic slogans warning against Islamic threats.

For their part, a number of western historians have been trying to rehistoricize, more intensively around the 900th anniversary of the first *crusade,* a designation that has almost become a generic expression for a zealous campaign. This crucial work, which undoubtedly contributes to the healing of memories, is hardly matched when it comes to reading the history of Muslim peoples. Worse, reductionist approaches that propose the notion of *jihad* as the key and the only key to interpreting Muslim attitudes towards non-Muslims, past and present, seem to receive a wide audience.

Thus many Muslims overstate the religious character of political and military confrontations, while many Christians, in the West but not only in the West, fail to historicize jihad and recognize its religious significance not only as legitimizing a defensive war but as the spiritual struggle in the way of God.

In addition to noting war-prone attitudes and fears fostered by the tendency to globalize Christian-Muslim relations, one could point to the way in which in the West the rights of Christian minorities are often advocated in predominantly Islamic countries, and the call for reciprocity in the treatment of minorities is frequently heard in religious and sometimes secular circles.[6] Religious communities have borrowed from states the logic of reciprocity, which favors a worldview that opposes an Islamic *ummah* with Christendom (no matter if both are not realities in the present time), each having a ramification in the abode of

---

[6] One example of this call, often said but not officially stated, was a Christian document drafted by the "Islam in Europe" committee. It was debated in 1996 and 1997 among Christians and Muslims from Europe and the Middle East and was subsequently revised. In recent years, a number of religious leaders spoke publicly the language of reciprocity, although official church texts, such as the pastoral document on relations with Muslims issued in 1998 by the Catholic Bishops Conference in France, de-emphasize this notion.

the other. Asymmetrically diverse, minorities can be and are perceived as victims and not actors. Their ability to act as bridge-builders is severely jeopardized when they are forced into a condition of hostages.

Many do continue to play this mediation role, but it is further put at risk when human rights violations are addressed selectively. Many of the interests of Christian minorities cannot be safeguarded and promoted except in conjunction with those of the Muslim majorities among whom they live. Upholding the rights of Christians in the Muslim world in a way that suggests foreign intervention for the sake of their protection reinforces the perception that they are alien in their own countries, or disloyal to those countries.[7] Defending the rights of Christians in opposition to their Muslim co-citizens and neighbors, with whom they share culture and national identity, aggravates the suspicion of majorities toward minorities because such a defense is seen as an instrument of a real or potential threat instigated by foreign and powerful forces.

Moreover, in some cases the amplification of a number of real problems faced by Christians may in fact hide an unwillingness to contribute effectively towards their solution. It may instead provide justification for a policy of resignation announcing the imminent eradication of the minorities.[8] What is then seen as an irreversible process renders the Muslim world homogeneous, a radical other, which can then be cast into outer darkness.

THE RIFT OF MANY NATIONS

In some parts of the world, the traditional nation-state model is subject to increasing questioning. Some countries, such as the Balkans, have fallen apart; others, such as in western Europe, are constructing larger entities. States have become too small for some purposes and too large for others. It is often claimed that the future belongs to the infranational and supranational formations. In many independent post-colonial countries of Africa, the Arab world, and Asia, nation-building projects remain incomplete, become fragile, or are failing. This is also the case in post-Soviet countries. The conflict in Chechnya, for instance, represents a potential shattering of the ever-fragile post-Soviet federalism as much as it reflects the possible advance of politicized Islam in Eurasia.

The borders set by the old and new imperial powers, while mostly unchanged, could not gain universal acceptance. In some cases they are

---

[7] This explains, for example, the virulent reactions in Egypt against the initiatives of the (official) US Commission on International Religious Freedom.

[8] See Jean-Pierre Valognes, *Vie et Mort des Chrétiens d'Orient* (Paris: Fayard, 1994).

disputed. Claims to common nationhood have been countered by the fact that ethnic, cultural, and linguistic communities sometimes straddle several state boundaries, while contributing to divisions within them. The examples are many in the Caucasian and trans-Caucasian regions and in the Balkans. National governments are often far from having succeeded in delivering on promises of genuine national independence and social and economic advancement. Indeed, in many instances, early progress has gone into reverse and large sections of the national population have sunk deeper into poverty. This has provoked or fueled many violent upheavals in Algeria, and in quite a few sub-Saharan African countries. Official rhetoric of development, national unity, democracy, and human rights often contrasts with realities and has contributed to erosion of the credibility of political institutions and their legitimacy.

The state is further weakened by a continuing globalization of economic processes and of information, which is associated with greater human mobility through migration, refugee movements, and the growth of transnational networks. The threat posed by a global culture to national and local identities adds to pressures on national and regional loyalties. New relations among people across traditional ties and webs of interest have created new loyalties and identities in which the local community has little meaning.

As many states are becoming weak, people are thrown back to identify with and rely for meaning and security on traditional community structures and identities. Conversely, when a state becomes oppressive, people find protection in traditional community structures and identities. In both cases, the effects of globalization leading to greater cultural uniformity in many cases invite a search for specificity and favor a reaffirmation of traditional identities. We are in the midst of a paradox: unprecedented homogenization exacerbates the quest for distinction and recognition.

When various human needs—personal and collective, material and symbolic—are being met or expressed in one identity instead of many, the borders between communal loyalties are mutually reinforced. Boundaries between oneself and the other are thus strengthened. They create closed communities within which common and exclusive memories can be developed and activated; the self and stranger are stereotyped, and the latter is easily demonized.

In such cases, differences in community size become an issue of minority threatened by majority. Insecure communities in one location seek alliances with others elsewhere who are perceived to share a common identity, in order to achieve political empowerment. National governments and political movements that are part of "majority" communities see their suspicion towards "minorities" justified and deepened. At the same time, some governments strengthen their power by managing communities and relations between them; exploiting mutual fears, mobilizing one against the other, and recruiting some in support, they thus further undermine the security of others.

In many countries the logic of politics and culture seems to go the way of national fragmentation. The dynamics of globalization limit substantially the exercise of power within the limits of a national territory. But this does not mean the universal demise of politics driven by national aspirations and considerations of national sovereignty. In fact, some countries manifest an awakened nationalism. But a widespread interpretation in the West based on a cultural or primordialist understanding of the nation considers nationalism an archaism, something like a return of history. At best, it is a late and disordered construction that in many societies is still thought to be the way of access to modernity.[9] Politicians invoke a world to be ruled by the universal principles of market economy, democracy, and human rights, but which is threatened by ancestral hatred. The problems of nationalism are seen as belonging to the realm of affectivity rather than that of politics. It is true that most of the protagonists in conflicts invoke history. Collective memories, once reactivated in political mobilization, may aggravate the temptation to think with the blood. But the success of such mobilization is not determined by ancestral atavisms but by political strategies of power conquest or preservation. It is not that ancestral hatred causes wars, but that war causes hatred. Ancestral hatred is, more often than not, fabricated rather than inherited. It is in many ways a creation of modernity more than an expression of a continued history.

DE-GLOBALIZING TENSIONS AND CONFLICTS?

It is undeniable that relations between Muslims and Christians are strongly influenced by local and regional histories and events. But, as suggested in this article, broader developments also have a significant impact, especially when they contribute to the destabilization of societies previously characterized by peaceful relations and shared life. In situations where uncertainties of change begin to be felt, mistrust and mutual apprehension can build up between communities and create tensions leading to conflicts.

When communities are identified or identify themselves exclusively by their religion, situations become more explosive. Christianity and

---

[9] Jacques Rupnik, *Le déchirement des nations* (Paris: Éditions du Seuil, 1995), 19–20.

Islam carry, though in different ways that are specific to region, deep historical memories. They appeal, although variably, to universal loyalties. They come to be seen as causes of conflict while often they are only an intensifying feature of disputes whose main causes are outside religion.

A conflict in one place, with its local causes and character, is sometimes perceived to be part of and instrumental to a conflict in another place, with its own separate and specific causes and character. So enmities in one part of the world spill over into situations of tension in other regions. An act of violence in one place is used to confirm stereotypes of the enemy in another place or even to provoke revenge attacks elsewhere in the world. What is otherwise a remote conflict becomes a local problem. Neighbors hold each other accountable for the wrongs attributed to their coreligionists elsewhere. Unless they are prepared to disassociate themselves publicly from those with whom they share a common faith, they are accused of complicity with them.

It is therefore crucial to offer a proposal that counteracts the process that tends to globalize conflicts involving Muslims and Christians. In other words, a vital step toward resolving Christian-Muslim tensions is de-globalizing them. Attention to the specific local causes of conflicts helps identify solutions to be found, first and foremost, in addressing those local causes. This is not possible unless the leaders of both communities refuse to be drawn into the conflicts of others on the basis of uncritical response to calls for solidarity among adherents to one faith. Only in applying common principles of peace, justice, and reconciliation will those party to local conflicts be helped to release Islam and Christianity from the burden of sectional interests and self-serving interpretations of beliefs and convictions. Christian and Islamic beliefs and convictions can then constitute a basis for critical engagement with human weakness, and with defective social and economic orders in a common search for human well-being, dignity, social justice, and civil peace.

In responding to these necessities, Muslims and Christians learn that Christianity and Islam are not two monolithic blocs confronting each other. In dialogue with each other "they understand justice to be a universal value grounded in their faith and are called to take sides with the oppressed and marginalised, irrespective of their religious identity. Justice is an expression of a religious commitment that extends beyond the boundaries of one's own religious community. Muslims and Christians uphold their own religious values and ideals when they take a common stand in solidarity with, or in defence of, the victims of oppression and exclusion."[10]

---

[10] Tarek Mitri, ed., *Striving Together in Dialogue: A Muslim-Christian Call to Reflection and Action*, no. 28 (Geneva: Office on Interreligious Relations and Dialogue, World Council of Churches, 2001).

What I find moving [in the text of John 4:5–19] is to see Christ, a Jew, not only talking to a Samaritan woman, but also holding a conversation with someone who has already had five men in her life and is now living with the sixth.

I remember half-a-dozen women coming to see me in my house one day. "Dom Hélder," they said, "we've no right to be here. We're fallen women. We live in the red-light district. We haven't come to discuss our spiritual problems with you. We've come because we're going to be turned out of the brothel quarter and moved somewhere terribly far away. Even where we are now, we find it terribly hard to make a living. If we have to go further away, we won't be able to make a living at all. Dom Hélder, we know you may be willing to stand up for us. You see, we've got no one to stand up for us."

I was immensely moved by the confidence these unfortunate sisters of ours put in me. We call them "sinful women." Sinners! As if we don't all of us have our sins, all of us have our own weaknesses. In our country they are also often known as "daughters of joy." But what a hard time they have of it. I was thrilled by the confidence they showed in me, by asking me to stick up for them....

So I said, "Before I give you my answer, I want to show you something written in the Gospel." And I took the verse where it says, "The prostitutes will precede you into the Kingdom of Heaven." What about that!

Dom Hélder Câmara
Through the Gospel with Dom Hélder Câmara

5 | *Peace and justice*
A theological hermeneutic
through one African woman's eyes

MERCY AMBA ODUYOYE

In 1988 the Central Committee of the World Council of Churches called the member churches of the council to stand in solidarity with women. Halfway through the designated decade,[1] it was clear that it was not going to be a decade of churches for women, but one of women for churches, or at best a decade of women for women and a decade for further emphasis on the justice and compassion for all that women have always stood for. Indeed, justice demands that women themselves find fullness of life in their communities. The recent non-government organizations (NGO) forum held in Huairou, China, demonstrated African women's passion for justice and peace.[2] Events in the recorded history of the continent demonstrate African women's participation in the search for peace with justice. This focus now informs the theological reflections of African women.

Looking at the world, Africa, and their immediate communities from the perspective of the righteousness of God has meant that African Women in Theology (AWIT) apply a hermeneutic of peace with justice in their reflections. They interpret women's experiences from the standpoint of what brings peace, well-being, shalom with justice, right-

---

Mercy Amba Oduyoye is director of the Institute of Women in Religion and Culture at Trinity College in Legou, Ghana, and is a native of that country. Professor Oduyoye has also served as deputy general secretary of the World Council of Churches, Geneva, and has lectured worldwide. Her books include *Hearing and Knowing*, *The Will to Arise*, *Daughters of Anowa*, *Socialization through Proverbs*, *Sons of the Gods and the Daughters of Men*, and *With Passion and Compassion*.

[1] This decade was launched on Easter in 1988. For a description of the history and events of this ecumenical project, see Mercy Amba Oduyoye, *Who Will Roll the Stone Away? The Ecumenical Decade of the Churches in Solidarity with Women* (Geneva: WCC Pubns., 1990).

[2] The forum was held 4–15 September 1995, parallel with the Fourth United Nations World Conference on Women held in Beijing. This conference was seen as more effective than previous conferences. There was some controversy about the fact that the NGO forum was moved to Huairou, outside Beijing.

doing righteousness. When they confront the absence of shalom, they seek transformation that will bring healing to the whole community without victimizing or oppressing any sector of the community, and without doing violence to the environment. In this offering, I present some of the experiences, both historical and contemporary, that have led AWIT to this theological locus. We shall review how this hermeneutic is applied to the church and seek to reflect on the signs of hope for transformation in both church and society.

As indicated in the title, this is a personal statement, but it has been reached as a result of my involvement in several theological communities, especially in the Circle of Concerned African Women Theologians (The Circle). The Circle was formed by AWIT in October 1989 to be a locus for theological reflection on African women in religion and culture. Its theological hermeneutic has been described by Musimbi Kanyoro, a founding member, as that of culture. The hermeneutic of culture is a tool that is slowly attracting the attention of people seeking alternative theologies that will be liberating, empowering, and life-enhancing, theologies to transform human experience so we can begin to see the answer to our prayer, "Thy will be done on earth as it is in heaven." AWIT has identified African culture as a reality with influences that are powerful in shaping life in Africa: the participation and experiences of women, the impact of Christianity, and the interaction of gospel and culture in Africa. Our position is that an understanding of African religion and culture is crucial for the quest for justice and fullness of life for all. This presentation emphasizes the quest for peace with justice, one of the aims of a transforming theology, and a particular concern of mine.

The recent UN conference on women held in Beijing demonstrated once again how economics rules the development of human communities and of nations. The NGOs from Africa as well as the delegates to the conference turned the floodlights on health, education, training, and participation of women. Economic Structural Adjustment Programmes (SAP), economic injustice, legal and political struggles were central to the women's agenda. The women's intensive analysis of the operations of multinationals and the globalization of all aspects of human interaction shows a process of de-development, a far cry from the vision of development that was the inspiration of the struggles for political independence in Africa. There was but one parameter of analysis that was not generally shared, that of the power relations between men and women. This was not on the conference agenda, whereas African women who presented workshops and plenary input at the NGO forum found the issue most critical. Herein lies the absence of peace, well-being, the shalom to which AWIT calls attention.

WHERE IS PEACE IN AFRICA?

The struggle for political independence from western powers and the struggle against apartheid and racism have so occupied Africa that almost no room is left for a gender-based analysis of life on the continent. Women were an integral part of the search for political justice as long as the antagonists were the colonial and neocolonial powers. Black Africans as a whole are faced with a situation in which their very humanity seems to be in question. The "anthropological poverty" of which the late Engelbert Mveng of Cameroun spoke is a reality and one that has its roots in colonialism and economic exploitation of Africa by its northern neighbors, including those of the Arab world.[3] It is also undeniable that the integrity of the human race is the underlying issue of peace with justice, not only in Africa but globally.

The economic policies being implemented on the continent benefit a tiny percentage of the population, the rich countries that have invested in Africa, and those who have investments with the banks that make loans to African governments. Economic justice seems to be defined by the world's financial institutions (World Bank and International Monetary Fund) as getting the maximum profits for their financial investments. It has nothing to do with adequate compensation for the labor of Africans who mine, farm, and fetch and carry to make the system work. Africa continues to be the source of human and material resources for the benefit of all who come to exploit. In Africa we cannot speak of economic justice except to speak of its absence. It is in addition to this general exploitation that is the lot of the Black African that one places the injustice done to women.

Wars and conflicts that have their roots in political and economic struggles continue to rage in Africa. Countries that do not have continuous combat have outbursts over economic deprivation and religious intolerance. Standing armies consume large proportions of national budgets and are maintained for the sake of a national security that often militates against the freedom of nationals. This militarism and militarization benefit the nations and peoples that produce and deal in weapons of war. Peace is a stranger to such conditions. How will people know well-being when their homes and farms continue to be a battleground? When religion and politics continue to generate conflict,

---

[3] Mveng was an art expert, clergyman, and historian who wrote on the themes of liberation and justice for South Africa and the wider world. He was murdered in 1995.

the peace of the whole community is put on hold. Moreover, since for African women peace is not the same as the cessation of militarism, peace is elusive in or out of war zones and refugee camps.

Civil society in Africa must struggle continuously to create environments that nourish peace. Voluntary organizations (my alternative for NGOs), mainly those of students, women, and trade unions, try to keep exploitation at bay and bring in shalom. The periodic protests of university students are against injustice, global and national, often those deemed to be perpetrated against themselves and the educational structures that affect them. When African women mobilize themselves, it is usually against injustices associated with decisions that affect women directly: population, reproductive rights, and legislation affecting traditional marriage customs and practices. When West African market women become vocal or close markets in order to take to the streets, their goal is to show their opposition to the inept attempts of a government to use price control to meet the challenges of economic management, or to curb the excesses of traditionalists who want to use culture for self-serving interests.

In recent years, women have been known to organize to ensure their participation in political structures. They have become more pro-active and, as was demonstrated at Huairou, they have embarked on education for democracy and for participation in politics. Peace movements have not become a style of involvement in Africa, but recently one hears more of the overt presence of human rights activists. In Africa, the best-known contemporary women's movements are professional and religious. African governments have promoted national councils for women's development, and a couple of first ladies have spearheaded social movements for the improvement of women's lives. Both Christian and Muslim women have unions to promote ethical precepts of their religions among women and girls and to be movements for containment rather than for transformation. All these groups tend more toward a philosophy of improvement rather than of justice and transformation that can nourish a life-giving peace. Several of these groups, especially the religious ones, deliberately counsel against confrontation, thus ensuring a peace without justice. Their daily struggles are for survival and these tend to leave root causes untouched. If peace is a state of lack of war and protest movements, then African women can be said to be at peace in many countries.

HISTORY'S LESSONS

Women's organizations have always been a part of societal structures in Africa, and they have served to ensure that women's perspectives are not overlooked. This provision for expressing political opinion is well-rooted in traditional structures of several ethnic groups in Africa. The fundamental principle is one of complementary structures and consultation of all interest groups on issues that affect the whole society. What follows here illustrates how these traditional provisions came into conflict with colonial procedures that regularly neglected to consult women. They are excerpts from the "Report of the Aba Commission of Inquiry Appointed to Inquire into the Disturbances in the Calabar and Owerri Provinces" in December 1921.[4] This event has been the subject of much study by scholars interested in women's roles, participation, and political status in Africa. It is chosen as a model of the socio-religious cultural situation that informs the theological reflection of AWIT because of the elements of a liberation struggle that these women embody. The event is an important part of the book of life through which God speaks to us. The account here is based on the report published in 1930 by the Government Printer in Lagos. With this tool, I attempt to portray how African women have acted and can act for peace with justice.

The commission interviewed several eyewitnesses, both nationals and colonials. The report gives no indication that any woman spoke directly to the commissioners. The language about the women was condescending. For instance, speaking of previous demonstrations by women, it was said that "It was no new phenomenon for the Ibibio and Ibo women of Calabar and Owerri provinces to organise, take direct action or make mass demonstrations," as if to say, no attention needs to be paid to them. In April/November 1925, the Danang Women's Movement came to the attention of the colonial administration. In April 1926, Calabar experienced what was a political movement, pure and simple. That is, the women refused to pay new tolls imposed at the market, on the grounds that "they had not been consulted nor the rule explained." In November 1927, a spiritual movement among women in the area seemed to pose a threat to peace. The British administration was forced to negotiate.

In the negotiations that followed, it became clear that the influence of women in the Ibibio (Efik) social system was far greater than had been supposed and that they did not lack eloquent and forceful leaders. In the investigation, some of the recent history of women's protests against westernization of their society was recalled. One women's uprising began in 1925 with a message received from God to return to ancient customs. The movement became anti-Christian and anti–British colonial

---

[4] This document, and other documents not specifically cited, are part of a collection of artifacts available to me as the director of the Women's Centre Trinity College.

administration. The movement of 1927 was "anti-pagan" and originated among the adherents of the Kwa Ibo Mission in the Uyo district and spread to other areas, affecting both men and women. The report has it that "It degenerated into a movement for the discovery and exorcism of witches during the course of which atrocities were committed," and that "drastic action had been taken." It was in fact an "unconscious return by many of the mission adherents to the original principles of katharsis—cleansing—and opening of the inner vision." This method of periodic cleansing of the body politic, in order to reestablish life-sustaining relationships with God, the ancestors, and among human beings, remains in use as part of the religious culture of Africa. This, in the view of AWIT, is an important element for theological reflection in Africa.

Part of the report indicates that the secretary of the southern provinces (an officer of the colonial administration) submitted a memorandum in which he wrote, "At the beginning of the dry season women are in a more neurotic condition than at other seasons and consequently are more liable to break out into disorder." Such are the sexist myths that greet women's concerns and protests. Hence the study by AWIT of the language about women as well as the hold of culture on women's lives. Noteworthy also is the fact that the message from God in 1925 included demands for increase in childbearing through improved sanitation, closer regard for certain customs, and a reduction in prostitution. The old customs were spelled out: men should leave the planting of cassava to women; the style and quantity of clothing to be worn by women was to be regulated; the use of European coins was interdicted; prices of foodstuffs in the market were to be regulated; cases should be tried in the villages and not in the "native courts" set up by the British colonial administration; dowries should not be expensive and should be paid in brass rods or native currency; married women should not be allowed free intercourse with other men.

The women then put out a report that all Europeans had left or were leaving. The intention is clear: the alien influences emanating from Christianity and British administration were felt to be oppressive forces that did not augur well for women and for the future of Africa. The rumor that all Europeans were on their way out was therefore a liberating word. The women were saying, "Get rid of these inimical influences and we shall be ourselves once more." AWIT is examining this claim against the competing claim that Christianity has lifted the African woman out of a state of total degradation. The colonial report blames Christian missions for teaching "equality and brotherhood, …a doctrine which is so foreign to the native,… misunderstood by him…, [with the] disastrous effect of breaking away from authority." The overt racism and the ignorance of African culture manifested here need no comment. It is necessary, however, to tease out the implications for Christian theology, especially the theology of religions. The missiological import is also obvious. That the women's protest was belittled is also clear. All of these are crucial for African women's theology.

Other parts of the report put the blame on mission schools, saying they have done far more than anything else to break down the control by native law and custom. The women's slogan stated in paragraph 56 of the report is pregnant with a mixture of religion and politics. Opposing taxation, they asked, "Why should the trees which bear fruits be taxed?" Motherhood and mothering roles continue to be the final court of appeal in Africa when dealing with issues of the humanity of women. What gives life, what is life-giving and life-sustaining, is the yardstick for measuring worthiness. African myths, legends, folktales, and proverbs are a rich source for concepts that inform African culture and are germane in constructing theology in Africa.

THE STRUGGLES OF TODAY

Manifestations of women's struggles for justice and respect for their humanity have continued to this day. Women in Africa's history, such as Nehanda of Zimbabwe, and women in contemporary Africa, such as the Black women of Soweto, have become models of women's resistance to dehumanization. Their concern is the survival and dignity of the African in the midst of global exploitation arising from colonialism and racism. Women have remained sensitive to injustices involved in being forcibly integrated into the culture of Europe without regard for what Africans see as the depths of true humanity.

When African men have gone along with westernization because it releases them from traditional obligations to women and the community life, African women have not hesitated to challenge them. That Mrs. Otieno lost her lawsuit against her late husband's family is a warning that African women cannot afford to be complacent about how, in the final analysis, African culture functions to the advantage of men. Women have not had much success using the traditional methods because the new and the modern, the westernized structures of decision-making, while more acceptable to the Euro-American world, consistently exclude women. Political power in Africa is a man's game, as is the power of religion. The exclusion of women from these arenas is a theological issue.

There are also areas of current interpretations of African culture that do not do justice to women; but for the sake of domestic and national "peace," especially the former, people in Africa, both women and men, prefer to ignore them. These issues are deemed to be potentially community-dividing. This studied neglect of what needs to be discussed and debated has created an atmosphere of peace without justice, daring any woman to be so awkward as to raise them. A few individual women have voiced the unease publicly by resorting to lawsuits and statements, at great personal risk. Some women's groups on university campuses have begun raising their voices. The most recent case of the violence against property and people related to Dr. Isabel Phiri of the University of Malawi is a case in point. Her "crime" is that she made public the findings of research into sexual harassment on the campus.

Generally, however, women's movements are cautious in their protest against moves to whittle away traditional expressions of women's authority by reinforcing and increasing women's disabilities and increasing the obstacles on their way toward the full expression of their humanity. The NGO forum of Beijing/Huairou demonstrates this caution. Herein lies the challenge of a cultural hermeneutic for the AWIT: How does one fence the internal critique of one's culture from becoming an excuse for racist exploitation? African culture needs transformation, but so do all human cultures. The challenge of solidarity is itself a theological issue.

Networking on a global scale in a liberating theology is a challenge to all who believe in the transforming power of the gospel of Jesus the Christ. The ecumenical movement has become such an instrument. The World Council of Churches (the movement I know best) has become a vehicle for promoting the liberative impulses embedded in the gospel. It has made itself available as a focal point for pulling together what the churches and movements related to the Christian religion (and others) are saying and doing on the questions of justice, peace, and the integrity of creation. It has turned attention on women by seeking a creative follow-through of the UN emphasis on women by urging the churches' solidarity with women. If covenants for peace and justice among human beings and with creation could be implemented, we might yet see justice and peace on earth.

AWIT expects the churches in Africa to become advocates for women. The ecclesiology they present requires this of the churches. It is true that the churches need to rid themselves of their own sexism, but we cannot wait for them to be perfect before Christians speak and act in favor of justice and peace. Eschatological hope informs all that AWIT does and says.

WOMEN AND CHURCH

Church women and church women's organizations have not yet begun to use traditional African methods to get the churches to act toward justice and peace in Africa. If the churches were fully aware of and concerned for the agenda of humanization and the integrity of the human community, their educational concerns would broaden out to include much that is left undone but which if done would promote justice and peace. The concern for a dynamic peace and justice is far from the center of the programs of churches in Africa. A clearer vision of education for justice and peace is a crying need, which until recently none in Africa seemed about to meet. Yet through the churches' participation in education, the making of human beings, the good news of Christian anthropology, could permeate the African continent. A domesticated, immobile church can quickly become irrelevant to women who are aware of the full dignity of their human being. It is becoming clear that women who would like to voice their critique of the church do not do so under the auspices of church women's groups. Neither do those who would challenge traditional practices that brutalize women.

The challenge to the churches in Africa is to liberate the church and its theology from aspects of cosmic religiosity, whether African, Hebraic, or Greco-Roman, that continue to be used as weapons against women, the poor, and the powerless. What AWIT aims at is to encourage church women to organize themselves to get involved in shaping the churches' agenda. No longer shall it be said that the problem with women is that we give money and voluntary labor to the churches, but then relinquish our share of the control of what they do and say. When women admit that they constitute the other in their churches, they will begin to challenge the churches' complicity in promoting a religion of comfort and acquiescence that becomes a tool of governments and business, or is simply passed over as irrelevant to the issues of the day. The church in South Africa has clearly demonstrated what the churches could be in Africa. It named the sin of racism and generated power to face it. The church in Africa could generate a movement against sexism if it were convinced that sexism is a sin. Faced with apathy towards sexism, AWIT has to generate theological resources for dealing with sexism in the churches in Africa. The dynamic role of South African women in the struggle against racism is evidence that African women are capable.

Feminists in other parts of the world identify men as the responsible agents and beneficiaries of sexism, but it is women's loyalty to a false peace and a false unity that has maintained the outer calm in which it flourishes. This can be illustrated in Africa, as elsewhere, in the training of children, brought up to fit into a patriarchally ordered world.

AWIT and other African women have also exposed the injustice of the plight of widows. The church is called to act effectively for justice and humanity where this specific issue is concerned. It has become a case of women being unable to extricate themselves from ritual observances riddled and shrouded with threats of disaster and death. "Who benefits from these rituals?" AWIT asks. Yet observing how these rites bring calm to the whole community, one treads softly. But we have not ceased to ask whether the recovery needed by all after the loss of a husband cannot be achieved otherwise.

In recent times, Euro-American women have made public the practice of female genital mutilation in parts of Africa. In the communities that have this practice, there is no unanimity as to its value and the need for it. And yet the fact is that in places like Kenya, African women had been struggling against this long before the contemporary feminist movement. Publicity over ritual practices has not been African women's strategy until recently. It was with shock and surprise that I watched Somali women expose the practice on Canadian television. History and contemporary experience attest to what African women can do in the face of injustice. The workshops at the NGO forum are further evidence of the dynamism of African women. Theirs is a power that stimulates African women's theology. The hope for transformation is the strongest hook on which AWIT hangs its theology.

In most parts of Africa, the church has yet to recognize the negative issues around and inside it. The new religious movements exploit the distress of the people, blaming their dire straits on Satan and other evil spirits. Other analyses are discouraged except those anchored on laziness and lack of faith. The church in Africa has not looked at itself in the mirror of Christ and therefore remains unaware of how it appears. When the churches undertake this self-examination we shall find more evils of which to repent. We shall see our divisions and turn to embrace the other against whom we had operated our -isms. We are in a depressed situation in Africa today not only because of economic problems, patriarchal structures, social and cultural strategies, and what we consider normative, but most radically because we refuse to empower the other to be a partner in shaping the changing values of our community life. With the burden/blessing of a triple heritage (African, Christian, Islamic), people in power are able to justify what is not just, generous, or life-sustaining for the other. The theological issues arising from this situation are those of empowerment, participation, and partnership. Can the church demonstrate *koinonia* to energize the community? AWIT locates its theology here and from this base calls for and seeks to be involved in transforming their relationships, praying, "Thy will be done on earth as it is in heaven."

WALKING TOGETHER

As women doing theology from the location described above, we have to develop a caring and supportive community solidarity as our survival strategy and what empowers our resistance and acts of transformation. Socialized to see ourselves as stabilizing agents of the community, we have to have a vision of what that community should be. We are taught that our education is for the education of the nation, but we have realized that the content makes for domestication and that the church reinforces this view. Given this context we cannot but expose the sexism that marginalizes, that uses women, whether it is in African culture or in the Christian church. We have had to take the veil off the church and expose its consent to promote the inadequate self-image that society imposes on women rather than living the gospel that liberates. The church has encouraged women to refrain from self-definition and to let their worth be determined by others. Women have been viewed as a means and sold ideologies of complementarity, apartheid, and other separate-but-equal philosophies that walk the road to separate-because-vastly-unequal. This education divorces justice from peace, and labels "peace" what should be called acquiescence in one's own oppression and marginalization. A hermeneutic of worthiness is at the root of African women's theology.

Justice and peace can walk together if African political and religious leaders come to admit that women and children are the worst sufferers in the state of continuous war and the devastating economic depression evident throughout the continent. The massive poverty that affects Africans is not only material. It is beginning to permeate the arena of ideas. We have become alienated from the traditional sources of wisdom, except to mine them for what promotes individualism and oppresses women. We have constantly pushed before us models of community and definitions of humanity that others have developed, and we have resigned from contributing intentionally and positively to global culture. Theologizing demands that we criticize our current experience. This AWIT has undertaken to do and to promote.

As African women, we are aware of what makes for our good. We are aware of sex tourism, we know prostitution, we know female genital mutilation, but we also know that these are not "women's issues" but injustices of the community to which women call attention. They are a challenge to the whole community of women and men, to be faced for the sake of justice in our contemporary life and for the sake of communal posterity. We know of modern legal systems that discriminate against women. We know what it would mean to have justice and peace, and to be treated as people who have a right to be involved in what affects their lives. But the day-to-day struggle to survive, the struggle to ensure that physical misery of hunger, nakedness, thirst, and homelessness are overcome, saps our energies. The struggle for survival is the African woman's cry for peace with justice.

A STRUCTURE OF INTERPRETATION

Christian theology has two fundamental sources, the Holy Scriptures and Life, that is, the world that God created and what derives from human culture. To extract meaning from life, those who have a theological interpretation resort to religion; their spirituality is fed with worship, liturgy, faith, and hope. Belief in a God of justice and compassion whose will is the shalom of all creation is the rock on which theology is to be founded. In *Daughters of Anowa; Talitha, 'Qumi!; The Will to Arise;* and other writings of AWIT, we meet women struggling with culture, religion, and their injustices. They expose the tools used for socialization toward the acceptance of a false peace and demonstrate how these are contrary to the mind of God. They are embarked on crafting a theology that challenges the justification of the oppression of women, children, the poor, and the powerless. They advocate solidarity for justice and urge our participation in justice-making. From the perspective of AWIT, justice is understood as God putting things right through human agency. Both the Bible and the traditions of the church are re-read from this standpoint.

Theological interpretation of what it means to be human is predominant in women's theology. These African women theologians ask questions about the meaning and implications of being created in the image and likeness of God. What is the blessing that distinguishes the human from other living beings? They call attention to human responsibility to care for life and to practice the generosity that is the nature of God. They point to the responsibility to create what is good and to let that increase and multiply on earth. If we believe ourselves to be co-creators with God, then under our management the world and all that is good should flourish. Anything short of this is injustice to the other with whom we share God's hospitality.

Justice and well-being are woven into the gospel of Jesus Christ. This good news involves making good what has been destroyed by sin and death. In the gospel we find what makes for the liberty of the children of God; we find caring, sharing, enabling people to live to their full potential. On the basis of this, AWIT identifies and challenges what does not make for shalom, and what forces uniformity on God's world, whose plurality and diversity God declared good. AWIT continues to ask, "What is the gospel?" in whatever situation its members reflect on.

Since the church continues to provide a home for many African women, AWIT's concern for justice makes them ask, "What is the nature of the new community that is generated from the life and teaching of Jesus of Nazareth?" AWIT is developing theological reflections around traditional themes of the reign of God, eschatology, and hope in the possibility of alternatives to the culture of death. They seek a resurrection from deadly structures here and now. They look for clues for transformation even where there seems to be none. Instead of the marginalization of women in the church, women propose from their re-reading of the Bible a discipleship of equals.

This hermeneutic of justice, or rather, of peace with justice, stimulates fresh approaches to traditional African and Christian principles of reciprocity, generosity, compassion, and the covenant of equals that should govern human relations. This is a theology en route, as all theologies should be.

A particularly effective way of helping the poor
to right the situation
is to encourage them to set up grass-roots communities.
For in these we find a community spirit
that lives on the gospel and draws its strength from Christ.
It is important that these communities should spring up
and get together in unity,
not in order to trample on the rights of others,
but to prevent others from trampling on their rights.

Experience shows that it is easy for the powerful
to crush, one, five or even ten people.
But no human force can crush a coherent community,
for it is a living God who dwells there
and listens to the outcry of his people.

Dom Hélder Câmara
Charismatic Renewal and Social Action: A Dialogue

6 | *Love and social transformation*
A reflection on base ecclesial communities in Latin America

JOSÉ MÍGUEZ BONINO

To be invited to participate in a Festschrift in honor of Dom Hélder Câmara (allow me to freely translate *Festschrift* as a festive testimony to celebrate his life and work) is both a privilege and a challenge. I met him personally only twice: first, for a long and active period at the Second Vatican Council and years later at the Free University of Amsterdam (Holland) which had conferred an honorary degree on him. Of course, I am not qualified to write about him: others have done so and do so in this Festschrift. My question is rather, what issues and questions should we address which would be relevant to Dom Hélder's life and ministry? At some point in his long and committed ministry he has addressed almost every significant issue of the relationship between faith and the social question. José de Broucker, one of his most perceptive biographers, has spoken about Dom Hélder's conversions: "From error to error, as he himself confesses, Dom Hélder's itinerary is made of successive conversions."[1] What, in this context, is the meaning of *conversion*? Is it a complete reversal, a 180-degree turn? Is it like the famous request a pope made of one of his theologians: "Refute what you once defended and defend what you once refuted"?

In part, Dom Hélder himself saw his conversions as being "from error to error." My interpretation, however, would try to move beyond this statement. I see Dom Hélder's itinerary as a permanent quest for

José Míguez Bonino is an ordained minister of the Argentine Evangelical Methodist Church (IEMA) and professor emeritus of the Higher Protestant Institute of Theological Studies (ISEDET), Buenos Aires, Argentina. In the course of his long career in theological education, Míguez Bonino lectured extensively and was a visiting professor at Emory University. He has received numerous academic recognitions, including honorary degrees. His most recent books are *Faces of Latin American Protestantism* (1995) and *Evangelio y poder* (1998).

[1] Hélder Câmara, *Las conversiones de un obispo: Conversaciones con José de Broucker* (Santander: Editorial Sal Terrae, 1980), 15.

new vehicles or new tools, which he discovered, transformed, and incorporated along a *caminhada*, a long journey, whose destiny, dynamics, and basic orientation remained the same. Using a line admirably developed by Erich Fromm, I see it as the road of a committed love which seeks awareness, understanding, commitment, cooperation, and efficacy.[2] Even more, in this quest certain basic dimensions remain the same. Dom Hélder Câmara's journey displays faith, somewhat ingenuous at times (I speak as a Protestant) in the human capacity for good, under the acknowledged and defended influence of Teilhard de Chardin's philosophical vision. It manifests commitment that chooses the condition of those in greatest need as a priority criterion. It shows trust in formative processes that can activate these potentialities (education at the base of society, in a happy encounter with Freire, the radio programs in the north, etc.). Finally, Dom Hélder's journey was characterized by a permanent search for ferments or yeast, minorities capable of leavening the dough.

His quest progressed from his errors (an integralism that placed excessive trust in the transforming potential of an ecclesiastical hierarchy) to his best findings, especially the base communities, "the Abrahamic minorities." The base community is perhaps what best brings together the spiritual, social, formative dimensions and the transforming dynamics that can nurture the people in the long journey toward full and universal humankind. Dom Hélder never thought of this universal humankind in terms of a territorial limitation, but as the point of arrival of the long and difficult trek to the "hominization" of creation. It is in this conviction, shared in Latin America by so many people, that I dare to offer this brief article.[3]

THE LOVE MOTIF IN LIBERATION THEOLOGY

Frequently in North Atlantic theology, Latin American liberation theology is perceived as predominantly or even exclusively concerned with structural, macro-social phenomena. It is a fact that concern for the poor and about poverty led to a macro-social analysis of class structure, the phenomenon of dependence, and the relations of production as an indispensable tool for theological reflection. However, careful consideration could have discerned from the beginning that this analytical work was a necessary instrument towards a better understanding of "the human condition" of the people, and was at the

---

[2] Eric Fromm, *The Art of Loving* (New York: Harper and Brothers, 1956).

[3] This paper does not intend to interpret the base communities in Dom Hélder's view or ministry, but to offer, from my own point of view, a socio-theological reflection on what they meant and mean in the quest for a new society.

service of "the salvific dialogue" (to use Gustavo Gutiérrez's language), which was seen as the mission of theology. As time has passed, the very experience of the struggle for social (structural) transformation has led to increased attention to the subjective (personal and communal) dimensions of that change. Recent literature (as early as the 1980s) clearly attests to this fact. But bear in mind that this is not a shift away from the earlier concern for social, economic, and political liberation. Rather it is a deepening of the personal, subjective, and intersubjective concerns, including ethnic, cultural, gender differentiation, which from the beginning found expression in the motifs of spirituality of poverty, personalization, celebration, and others.

In this paper I intend to explore this dimension by selecting a motif that has played a fundamental role in the language, experience, and spirituality of liberation theology, the love motif. This motif has been important in liberation movements even outside the direct presence of the Christian or any religious inspiration.[4] Naturally, such language becomes more central and intentional in the discourse of Christians participating in social movements. Here it appears as the deepest source of commitment. Hugo Assmann has framed, I think, the pertinent comment and question: "With respect to the rich experience in which the personal need to love and be loved is realized, what is the meaning of giving one's life for one's brother in the wider context of the historical process? Is there not a need to enlarge the parameters of our experiential references in our understanding of the gratuitousness of love?" And a little later: "Every attempt to discover a human motivation for the struggle for liberation sooner or later comes up against the need to inquire into the meaning of the radical praxis of dying for others.... This radical question is theological."[5]

These quotations come from the 1970s, when social conflict frequently had a military expression and the question of giving one's life or dying for others took on dramatic significance. Well-known "pacifist" liberationists including Dom Hélder Câmara and Adolfo Pérez Esquivel

---

[4] Anybody acquainted with Marx's harsh denunciation of Christian love as an obstacle in the proletarian struggle may be surprised that a confessed Marxist Leninist such as Ernesto (Che) Guevara would give love a central place in his thinking and would not hesitate to say that "a revolutionary is a person possessed by deep feelings of love" (Ernesto Guevara, *Obras completas* [Buenos Aires: Ediciones del Plata, 1967], 2:19, 24). Similar expressions can be found in other leaders of the Cuban or Nicaraguan revolutions. One could conceivably understand this vocabulary as a residue of a long-established Christian tradition or as a tactical use of a language that could evoke a response. Both explanations, however, would witness to the persistence of a deeply rooted Christian consciousness.

[5] Hugo Assmann, *Teología desde la praxis de la liberación: Ensayo teológico desde la América dependiente* (Salamanca: Ediciones Sígueme, 1973), 69, 76.

in Latin America; Martin Luther King, Jr., in USA; Nelson Mandela in South Africa; and many others were using the same language. They were experiencing the same dramatic and ever-present condition of risking their lives, and accepted it as an act of love and obedience in following Christ. At the dawn of the twenty-first century, in different but equally critical struggles, now against exclusion and marginalization, against insecurity and "white gloves" repression, the motif of love continues to be central for a committed Christian person, church, or community.

Nevertheless it is not my intention to reflect theologically on the significance of love in the struggle for social transformation but rather to explore the concrete meaning of that motif in the experience of the Christian communities committed to that struggle. I will refer specifically to the base ecclesial communities (BEC) which have played a decisive role in a renewal of the Roman Catholic Church but also in the larger society in which they are active.[6,7]

THE GOSPEL FOR THE NON-PERSON

Gustavo Gutiérrez has contended that while the goal of evangelizing in the North Atlantic world is to lead the secularized person to the acceptance of the existence of God, in Latin America it is to help the non-person to the awareness that God is their Father. The first part of the statement may or may not be correct; the second is undoubtedly right. The "non-person" is not an abstraction. It is the large masses of Latin American poor, the traditional poor as well as those who have become poor in the last decade of the twentieth century, including the growing number of the lower middle class let loose by unemployment. Their present economic condition is caused by specific economic developments related to the "new economic order" proclaimed by George Herbert Walker Bush at the end of the Iraq war, and usually identified as neo-liberal. These masses of "marginalized," "unnecessary" and therefore "undesirable" are the matrix of the "non-person." They reach to 60 or 70 percent of the "absolute" and "critical" poor of the United Nations (UN)

---

[6] Among many important sources on base ecclesial communities, probably the best interpretation from a theological perspective is Leonardo Boff's *Igreja, carisma e poder: Ensaios de eclesiologia militante* (Petrópolis: Vozes, 1981), chap. 9, 10. See also Sérgio Torres, ed., *A Igreja que surge da base: Eclesiologia das comunidades cristãs de base*, IV Congresso Internacional Ecumênico de Teologia, São Paulo, 1980 (São Paulo: Edições Paulinas, 1982).

[7] For purposes of clarity I will refer only to the classic base ecclesial community movement in the Roman Catholic Church (RCC) developed since the early 1960s, from Panama and Brazil, which extended all over the continent. Among Protestant evangelicals, some Pentecostal communities in particular display social characteristics and psycho-social traits similar to those of the BEC.

or Economic Commission for Latin America (CEPAL) statistics for Latin America. Part of these people have always been the poor of the land. As peasants in a semi-feudal system, or quasi slaves in the mines, or aborigines in their reservations, they were never given full human status. But now the uprooting from their traditional social context has given a new face to their alienation. Sociologists call it *anomie,* a condition in which the worldview, the values and norms that gave stability to individual and collective life, break down and people are left without shelter. Self- and social-identity, social relations, and ethical norms are shattered. A re-socialization, adaptation, or transformation of the person will have to take place; the primary socialization of the traditional society will co-exist, conflict with, or be displaced by this secondary socialization of the new world.[8] Although from different conditions, the new poor, whose pauperization comes from unemployment in the proletariat and the lower middle class, suffer a similar crisis. The question becomes: How can this recreated identity come about? Into which world? For what kind of society will this new birth take place?

This is the social and psychological locus where the question of evangelization has to be faced. In the new world where these people are located is a world of meanings, relations, roles, and self-understandings structured by the new characteristics of the capitalist globalized society; and by a culture sometimes called postmodern. Human beings are almost exclusively defined as producers and consumers in an arena of permanent competition. This world has few places for newcomers to become active participants in the race. The great majority will be seen as passive "stuff" to be used or laid aside as waste.

In this context we can look at the meaning of the BECs. It is not by chance that the country where BECs have seen greatest growth and influence is the one in which the church first understood and called attention to the new social conditions. In fact, the documents of the North-East Bishops Conference (Brazil) of 1973 included a detailed analysis of the economic conditions in the area, and the social situation

---

[8] The concept of *anomie* originated in 1897 with Émile Durkheim (*Le suicide: Étude de sociologie* [Paris: Presses universitaires de France, 1968], 263–311), and has been developed by R. K. Merton in "Social Structure and Anomie," *Social Theory and Social Structure* (Glencoe, Ill., Free Pr., 1957). For some critical observations concerning the potential conservative use of the notion, see Peter L. Berger, *The Sacred Canopy* (Garden City: Doubleday, 1967). For the ideas of primary and secondary socialization, see Peter L. Berger and Thomas Luckmann, *The Social Construction of Reality: A Treatise in the Sociology of Knowledge* (Garden City: Doubleday, 1967), especially chap. 3. Anthropologists Clifford Geertz and others have recently revisited and introduced corrections in these concepts.

and the consequences for the life of the people, particularly the poor and marginal. Dom Hélder Câmara concludes: "It seems that the time has arrived when people should see what is our mission as Church." He then quotes the synod's conclusion: "Listening to the cry of those who suffer violence and are oppressed by unjust systems and mechanisms and listening to this challenge, perverse and contrary to God's plan, we all discover together that the mission of the Church is to be present in the heart of this world, preaching good news to the poor, liberation to the oppressed and joy to the afflicted."[9]

The BEC represents another world, a new socialization with a different sign. The continuity with the old identity is preserved in a world of symbols deeply rooted in the Christian consciousness. But the meaning and operation of these symbols are radically transformed. The center of this transformation is the experience of the community of mutual love and solidarity. The love is experienced and exercised concretely in the communal appropriation of Scripture and the church, in sharing the sorrows and joys of everyday living, in commitment to and organization for the solution of the problems and needs of their own and the larger community.

Common celebration, reflection, and action are the cradle of a new personal identity. The new person claims and is given the word; they can speak and be heard. They become the subject of decision. God announces God's word in their reading and they respond to the word of the gospel. The Holy Spirit builds the *ekklesia* as they come and celebrate together. Thus, my personal identity is not created over against others but together with them. Social identity is not achieved by suppressing the individual (as in the mass) but by projecting and acting, praying and thinking together in freedom. We should not idealize the BEC. Competition, conflict, envy, indifference, and cheating are part of every human society. But the important thing is the universe of meanings and symbols in which the whole ambiguous process takes place. Personal self-realization and the building of a world are conceived and approached as a project of love, an active, responsible, constructive, and lucid love in which free reception of God's love and openness in trust to the neighbor presuppose and imply each other.

Can we not recognize in this experience the New Testament account of lostness and salvation? The transition from objective and subjective destruction (*phthoria*, meaning decay, corruption, death) to objective and subjective re-creation (new creature) takes place in both cases as the Holy

---

[9] Hélder Câmera, *El grito del Tercer Mundo en un pueblo marginado: ¿Milagro brasileño?: testimonios* (Buenos Aires: Merayo Editor, 1974), 107.

Spirit brings to life the word of Christ in the mutuality of love (*koinonia*) of the community of faith. Elizabeth Moltmann-Wendel[10] has noticed, in the context of an analogous process in the condition and the recovery of self respect of women, that this experience is at the subjective level that of the Reformation. It finds expression in the doctrine of justification by faith, and is understood as God's unqualified acceptance, what she calls "the matriarchal element of unconditional acceptance and love." This is precisely what liberation means, subjectively, for the poor. This is the experience of rebirth and new life in the BEC.

How is the good news of God's unconditional acceptance historically mediated to the non-person? We have almost exclusively relied on proclamation, usually understood as oral proclamation. But we know today that words gain meaning in terms of the language code and the accepted social relations and meanings. How can the message of unconditional acceptance be received unless a community of mutual free acceptance gives it a content, a content that can be extrapolated and that makes intelligible the word of free grace?

We are speaking here not of two different realities but of a single event, which needs to be lived and accounted for in two sets of propositions: "I am accepted by God" and "I belong in the community of love." New Testament studies have shown us clearly that such Pauline formulas as the Pauline "in Christ" (*en Christō*) must be understood in this sense, not as a mystical individualistic experience but "primarily as an ecclesiological formula."[11] The BEC is for the non-person the concrete historical locus where the experience of rehumanization takes place. To be "in Christ" is simultaneously and inseparably to have a personal relation with him from the Holy Spirit and to be in the community of love, to regain the dignity of a person who has received the word, who speaks and is heard, and who creates with others a project for himself or herself which is at the same time a historical project for society.

This personal/communal process is of paramount importance when we think about the structural process of social transformation. Are we, in our struggle for change, forced to choose between the capitalist technocratic so-called liberal democracies where human life is sacrificed to the objective mechanisms of the universally globalized market, and totalitarian socialism where a relative material welfare is bought with captivity to a rigid impersonal, bureaucratic and repressive "uniformiza-

---

[10] This quotation from Moltmann-Wendel, and those (below) from her husband Jürgen Moltmann, are taken from lectures they gave in April 1985 in St. Louis and San Francisco as part of a lecture tour organized in their honor.

[11] Rudolf Bultmann, *Theology of the New Testament* (New York: Charles Scribner's Sons, 1951), 1:311, and *passim*.

tion"? The historical project for which those in the Latin American struggles for social change have opted has to be characterized as a humanistic democratic socialism or a social democracy. But these goals cannot be reached automatically. In fact, a hardness inevitably develops in the struggle for change (not only when it takes the form of a revolutionary conflict); there is always the danger of a return of the old system in the form of a new authoritarianism. Here the only insurance for a real democracy is the active participation of a people who personally and collectively take on the socio-cultural project. In this sense the BECs are seedbeds of a humanistic democratic socialism or a social participatory democracy through the creation of self-aware people, who claim their place and right as active subjects of their own and their society's history. They exercise this right daily and conceive of it not as an individualistic isolated right but as a collective creation. In this sense the BEC is profoundly political, an experience of solidarity in Christian love which seeks expression in a secular political order congruent with the personalization-in-community it has experienced at the religious level.

IDENTITY AND MOTIVATION

In the language of Christians participating in the struggles for social change, love as motivation for social change takes the name of *solidarity*. This notion has, of course, a long and complex history. As a social and political concept it probably originates with the forerunners of the French Revolution and was taken up by Jean-Charles-Léonard Simonde de Sismondi and the French socialists. It is probably from there that it entered the language of the labor movement. On the other hand, it soon became a favorite concept among English Christian socialists, Swiss religious socialists such as Hermann Kutter and Leonhard Ragaz, and Roman Catholic social thinkers from the nineteenth century.[12]

Roman Catholic social doctrine has defined solidarity as an anthropological given, a basic structure of human existence. As such it is not merely a moral obligation but an ontological reality. Human beings are linked by virtue of their nature, which is both personal and social. On this basis one can speak of a "solidarity principle," defined as mutual inevitable interaction of the whole with the members and the members with the whole. Consequently we are to reject both an individualism that sees society only as the interaction of individuals, and a collectivism that denies personal identity and makes the individual a mere object of social projects. The principle of solidarity thus conceived, with the principles of

---

[12] See H. Weber, "Solidarität," in *Die Religion in Geschichte und Gegenwart*, 3rd ed. (Tübingen: J.C.B. Mohr [Paul Siebeck], 1962): 6:130–1.

the common good and of subsidiarity, constitute the framework for Catholic social doctrine. The ordering of relations and priorities in the articulation of these three principles usually distinguishes different schools. Some moral theologians, including Heinrich Pesch and Oswald von Nell-Bruening, have given a determining priority to the solidarity principle in what has been called *Solidarismus*. In the social thinking of the ecumenical movement, the idea of solidarity has been central in the notion of the responsible society, the focus of the social thinking of the World Council of Churches (WCC) between Amsterdam (1948) and Uppsala (1968). The word *solidarity* itself does not appear so frequently, but the notion underlies emphases such as "the unity of humankind," "the human community," and *Mitmenschlichkeit*.

It is not difficult to discover the presence of all these influences in the Latin American idea of solidarity as foundation and motivation for social and political action. But it would be a mistake to believe that the concept has merely been taken over or adopted from an ideology or doctrine or a combination of several of them. It is not, on the other hand, a question of originality or exclusivity. What interests us is how groups of Christians under the conditions of struggle for social change in Latin America live, understand, and define solidarity.

First, this solidarity is related to a specific historical situation. The Medellín conference put in this way: "To commit oneself is to actively ratify the solidarity in which every human being is immersed, assuming the tasks of human promotion in the line of a specific social project.... A commitment thus understood must be characterized in Latin America, in the peculiar circumstances of its present historical moment, by the sign of liberation, humanization and development."[13]

Thus, we are not speaking only of an ontological structure but of a praxis—an active commitment to a specific history. It is a situated solidarity. This entails choices. Medellín was also clear in this respect: "We must sharpen the awareness of the duty of solidarity with the poor, which love *(caritas)* imposes on us. This solidarity means to make our own their problems and struggles, to know how to speak to them" (14/10).

Love, therefore, means solidarity lived in the conflictive situation created where the poor suffer from and struggle against injustice, exploitation, and alienation. As Denis Goulet writes about the problems of underdevelopment and unjust world economic structure: "Given

---

[13] *La Iglesia en la actual transformación de América Latina a la luz del Concilio* (Second General Conference of the Latin American Episcopate, Medellín, 1968), 10/9. In this and subsequent references, numbers refer to the number of the document and the paragraph.

men's present dispositions, authentic solidarity...cannot be gained without serious conflict."[14]

We cannot simply adopt the notion of solidarity as developed within consensus models that presuppose the existence of a fundamental justice and therefore pursue a model in which social harmony is seen as achieved and taken for granted. Solidarity is not a given. It has to be built. Or perhaps it would be more correct to say that the ontological reality and the factual situation create an ethical demand. This has a twofold aspect. On the one hand, since present social conditions of marginalization and anomie tend to destroy or neutralize the sense of solidarity among the poor, it becomes necessary to develop concrete forms and channels to awaken, stimulate, and give expression and organization to that solidarity.

Traditional doctrine tended to see solidarity as an ontological structure and consequently to base it theologically on a concept of human nature related to the doctrine of creation and natural law. This approach is understandable against the background of classical Roman Catholic doctrine. But the dominant tendency in Latin American liberation theologies, as expressed not only or mainly in formal theological literature but also in liturgies, song, and spirituality, is to see solidarity in a christological and eschatological perspective. In its justly famous definition of peace as the fruit of justice and as a permanent task, Medellín concludes: "Peace is, finally, the fruit of love, the expression of a real fraternity among human beings, a fraternity brought about by Christ, the Prince of Peace, by reconciling all men to Himself. Human solidarity cannot be fully realized except in Christ who gives a peace that the world cannot give" (2/14 c).

This approach is frequently articulated more specifically: Christ realized in his own life and death God's solidarity with the poor and oppressed. He made himself one of them, sharing the full weight of their sufferings and death, and involves us in our solidarity with them: "Insofar as you have done it for one of these my little brothers, you did it for me" (Matt. 25.40). Thus, to follow Christ is to commit oneself to the cause of the poor. Eschatologically, solidarity is a commitment to a project that always seeks to anticipate proleptically the universal unity in justice and love of the kingdom. While historically committed, and therefore engaged in the conflicts of history, solidarity with the poor is not a static thing but has an inherent tendency to universalize itself, overcoming the structures and conditions that work against the

---

[14] Denis Goulet, *The Cruel Choice* (New York, Atheneum, 1975), 140.

solidarity of social classes, peoples, races, or sexes, drawing into it the whole humankind.[15]

How does this tension between a committed partiality and the universal intention of the solidarity of love impinge on the struggle itself? I will not enter here into the question of love and conflict or even love and violence, which has been frequently discussed and deserves careful attention. Rather I want to make now a different point, namely, how is personal and group identity perceived within a conflictive situation such as the one we have lived through and still suffer in diverse but interrelated ways. There always is, in such situations, a tendency to define our identity by opposition, as a function of the existence of the enemy. It would be illusory to believe that such a tendency can be eliminated. But there is clear evidence that it is not dominant in the communities of Christians committed to social transformation. While the image of the enemy is never absent (how could it be when oppressors are constantly pressing their project of violence and death on the poor?), the deeper identity is born in the encounter with the brothers and sisters who listen to me and speak to me, who sustain me to the point of laying down their life for me.

Opposition to the enemy is not an end in itself but a temporary and necessary function of the solidarity with the brother or sister who suffers. Thus, identity is not established primarily as exclusive but as inclusive: of the poor and oppressed outside the community (in the larger society), of the poor and oppressed engaged in struggles for liberation elsewhere in the world, and of the people from other social groups and classes who make an option for the poor and potentially for all as the conditions of oppression are overcome. There is at this point a particularly significant development in the last two decades: the increasing recognition and acceptance of ethnic and gender diversity which cannot be simply subsumed under the general category of poor. The recognition of particular struggles within the total quest for justice, and even of different political actions, are signs of this attitude which can already be seen in the BEC movement and in other forms of peoples movements.

"LOVE HOPES ALL THINGS.... LOVE NEVER ENDS"

The attitude, the theological penchant, dominant in the theology of liberation that developed with and is intimately related to the BEC has

---

[15] This universal note is particularly stressed in the life and message of Dom Hélder Câmara and appears at almost every point in his career and writings. He sees Latin America, and particularly his own ministry in his country and area, as inserted in the total task of "the Abrahamic minorities" and the total project of hominization of humankind.

been criticized for its optimism. Sometimes, particularly in European theological circles, it has been interpreted as a *theologia gloriae*. Critics see it as tied to a deficient eschatology that has not taken account of the gravity of sin. The somber events of the last twenty years seem to show the illusory character of the hopes for liberation and to invite a theology of resignation or an eschatological expectation fixed on a future life or an apocalyptic crisis. Military regimes accompanied by oppression and death have been replaced by weak and controlled democracies in which the state is unable to establish social policies and falls prey to an inhuman economic domination. The result is increased marginalization, hunger, sickness, and despair. It would be foolish to ignore or deny the seriousness of the situation and the critical theological questions it raises. I want to end by looking in the direction of our central theme to two aspects of an eschatology built on the evangelical assurance of the triumph of love.

The BECs' choice represents a theological perspective on political and social praxis that rests on hope that human beings, inspired by love of God and neighbor and committed to the good of the larger community, can awaken and strengthen a will to produce social change for the benefit of all. Of course, BECs are aware of human limitation and consequently of the need for permanent correction in quest of "the greater good possible." To buttress that hope theologians have frequently appealed to a restricted view of the consequences of the Fall in human nature, a remainder of an original nature on which social life can be built. Over against this position some Protestant theology, particularly in Europe, built on an anthropological pessimism, seems to rob political and social life of all eschatological density and considers it, at best, a remedial action to obtain "the lesser evil." Are we really forced to choose between an optimism resting on some precarious residue of original justice that survives sin, and an anthropological pessimism that is the social equivalent of a personal eschatology in which the one who dies is discontinuous with the one who rises in resurrection (obviously a heresy)? I think the theological dynamic of the BECs, built on the strength of a divinely given and divinely sustained love, opens a different perspective. BECs view the world and history as encompassed and permeated by the presence of grace and the power of the Spirit. The love that motivates active and committed solidarity is the love of the crucified Christ, who in the power of the Spirit presses towards full realization of the all in all, meanwhile opening in its way infinite new historical possibilities. Sin is seen not as a static quantity or an established obstacle to human accomplishments but as a negative force with which to engage in a permanent struggle: The quest for peace, justice, and freedom is a struggle that will endure until the end. The eschatological distance is not a pre-set limit to human creativity but an ever-moving target. Better, it is an absolute future that challenges us to discern the relative future struggling to be born in the womb of present reality. Love, which is the only absolute future and the only absolute opposite to sin, is the power that gives an insight into new possibilities and motivates the struggle for the greater good.

But what about death? Death is a constant presence in the struggle for justice and peace. It takes many forms: oppression, defeat, sickness, hunger and malnutrition, torture, unemployment, repression, and loss of loved ones. The life of the poor is a never-ending experience of death, subjective and objective, personal and collective, sudden and prolonged. How could eschatology be absent from a faith lived under the shadow of death? In fact, the eschatological dimension is central to the whole experience of spirituality and theology inspired by the BECs. Some brief references may give an insight into the ethos of that eschatological spirituality.

However we evaluate the concrete choice he made for armed struggle, Néstor Paz makes clear the connection between love, death, and hope in one of the final entries in his diary (1972):

> My dear Lord… You know I've always tried to be faithful to you…. That's why I am here. I understand love as an urgent demand to solve the problem of the other—where you are….
>
> Maybe today is my Holy Thursday and tonight will be my Good Friday. Into your hands I surrender completely all that I am with a trust having no limits, because I love you…—because you are my Father.
>
> Nobody's death is useless if his life has been filled with meaning, and I believe ours has been.
>
> Ciao, Lord, perhaps until we meet in your heaven, that new land that we yearn for so much.[16]

Two brief poems, frequently sung in BEC worship, one from Brazil and the second from Argentina, reflect this same attitude:

> Migrants
>
> The universe moves by the power of love,
> and the light of its stars lights my way.
> My work in communion will cause the rice fields
> to flower, soaked in streams of justice,
> and in their fruit we will gather freedom!

---

[16] Ed Garcia and John Eagleson, ed. and trans., *My Life for My Friends: The Guerrilla Journal of Néstor Paz, Christian* (Maryknoll: Orbis Bks., 1975), 87.

Zamba of the grain of wheat
Zamba of the seed of wheat,
tomorrow I shall be bread:
I'm not afraid of the furrow,
some day I shall germinate;
Silence and night in my grave,
while the ear germinates,
hundred percent and the milling:
tomorrow I shall be bread....

This is the experience I tried to convey in writing some years ago about eternal life:

> *There is no other answer to the question of life after death. It belongs to the same reality as this life. We have* one *life on this side of death—not a meaningless series of isolated moments or episodes—because of and in the extent to which we participate in the reality of love. And since love is not a mere human manifestation, but an overflow of feeling that has as an impetus and foundation* the very being of God, *life has an eternal future. The meaning of our life before death and our belief in a life after death has one single guarantee: the love of Jesus Christ. The love of God and our active acceptance of it constitute the only possibility for life to arise out of these series of disconnected, often contradictory thoughts and actions, triumphs and failures; and such a meaningful life must have a future in the afterworld. In love, and only in love does our life have a future.*[17]

Finally I would simply like to suggest three points at which I find fruitful this way of approaching eschatology from the experience of love and commitment.

In contrasting the Platonic idea of immortality of the soul and the Christian belief in the resurrection of the dead, Jürgen Moltmann has made a fundamental point: the distinction between the future of a lived life and the timeless eternity of an unlived life. He summarizes the meaning of the former in words that perfectly convey the experience I am trying to indicate: A lived life "is **full life before death**. They become mortal but their death is a fruitful and meaningful death. Dying, for them, is the ultimate giving of life, the perfect affirmation of life. They who 'lose' their life in this sense will 'find' it in eternity, because God resurrects the dead into the eternal life of his kingdom."[18]

In the lived eschatology of the BEC the unity of the present life, understood as a commitment of love to the liberation of the other, and the future life, understood as participation of God's kingdom of perfect

---

[17] José Míguez Bonino, *Room to Be People* (Philadelphia: Fortress Pr., 1979), 53.
[18] Ibid., 10.

love, are an indissoluble unity. Perhaps we arrive at the awareness of this unity in different ways. First in our hermeneutical circle is the lived reality of a shared commitment of love which bears the marks of its eschatological density. In more direct language, the community experiences the presence of the crucified and risen Lord in their midst as they live their daily life. That which is tasted as an aperitif cannot but awaken the hunger for the hope of the full banquet. On the other hand, in European theology, one usually starts with the promise, which draws the project to itself. But it is important to avoid a misunderstanding. We are in both cases speaking of God's free love in Jesus Christ. There is no case for contrasting an anthropological and a christological approach. Perhaps in one case the primary reality is the present awareness of God's love that opens the eyes to hope, and in the other it is the proclamation of the final victory that awakens the commitment of love. In any case, if this difference exists (I doubt that it does), it should not be exaggerated. It probably corresponds to the weight in our situation of an ecclesial praxis that is less determinative in the theological methodology of European theology. The important point is that we are speaking of the future of a bodily personal and collective life. This means, conversely, that we are speaking of the eschatological weight of the present bodily personal and collective life.

Another important consequence of this way of approaching eschatology from the experience of love as solidarity, hope, and commitment is that it breaks the dichotomy between a personal and a social eschatology. The question of personal identity that we discussed earlier is of fundamental importance here. Personal identity in the bourgeois world is conceived in terms of privacy, of self-affirmation in permanent competition. Eternal life, in this view, is the fulfillment of that vision: individualistic, private, and static. As J. B. Libânio ironically puts it: "A state of permanent satiety, from which every lack and anxiety have been excluded…, heaven becomes a kind of 'eternal television.'" In impersonal collectivism, personal identity is lost in collective identity. The future can therefore only be conceived as an ideal utopian future society. There is no place there for personal life after death except as realized in the species. This seems to be an insurmountable contradiction in Marxist thought, which Ernst Bloch has had the courage to acknowledge and had tried to face constructively within the limits of his interpretation of materialism.

In the experience of the BEC, personal identity and social commitment are a single process; my personal future and that of the project of solidary love are interwoven. In affirming the former, I simultaneously affirm the latter and vice-versa. My personal identity is not private property but an interpersonal reality, a gift of the community. Any who lose their life in this project of love will gain it, not as a result of arbitrary divine adjudication of rewards but because such a life has entered into a fellowship of life with the crucified and risen Lord and his friends which cannot be destroyed by death. While we cannot expect much theological speculation at this immediate base level, where the symbolic images of biblical eschatology are received immediately (though not literally), future personal life and the hope of the kingdom are inseparable. Significantly, when the names of the dead are called out in the BEC, the community answers, "Present!"

Finally, in the eschatological language of the BECs the apocalyptic evocation of judgment and punishment of enemies is relatively absent. Celebration of future freedom, overcoming exploitation and hunger, and victory over death and pain are featured, but the oppressor is scarcely mentioned. When the question is explicitly asked, mostly in historical rather than eschatological terms, the usual answer is that oppressors have been deprived of the power to oppress, or that they will participate in the common good.

It seems to me that this is the result of two things. On the one hand, the struggle is historicized rather than projected apocalyptically. In contrast to reactionary religious rhetoric, among BECs enemies are not viewed mythically but at a human level, where rational analysis can explain their attitudes. One frequently hears, even from simple people, that exploiters are themselves victims who need to be liberated. On the other hand, as I have insisted, the project is understood and lived as a project of solidary love, which is historically situated, but by its own nature universally open. If anything, this eschatology could be accused of *apokatastasis*.

As noted above, we should not idealize or romanticize the BECs. They share the human sin and weakness we know from the witnesses of the first Christian communities. But the life of this community movement is characterized by an ethos and a project that gives it coherence. I have contended that this ethos and project can best be articulated around the motif of love, which is the subjective side of the social and political activity of the communities, just as activity is the objective side of the ethos of love.

My personal vocation is to be a pilgrim of peace.
Personally I would prefer a thousand times more
to be killed than to kill anyone.
We need only to turn to the beatitudes—
the quintessence of the gospel message—
to see that the option for Christians is clear.
We are on the side of nonviolence
and this is in no way an option of weakness and passivity.
Opting for nonviolence means to believe more strongly
in the power of truth, justice, and love
than in the power of war, weapons, and hatred.

Dom Hélder Câmara
The Violence of a Peacemaker

The Good Samaritan today
would be dealing with the ever-growing number
of victims of injustice.
He would be here—he is here—
peacefully but boldly fighting
against the unjust structures
crushing the human race.
For it is not enough to help
the victims of evil.
Unacceptable evil
must be attacked at its roots.

Dom Hélder Câmara
Through the Gospel with Dom Hélder Câmara

7 | *Dismantling racism nonviolently*
A case study in practical theology

DANIEL S. SCHIPANI

The two preceding quotes express well the main feature of Dom Hélder's ministry and thought: his unique blend of concern and work for peace and justice. For he was, indeed, a "pilgrim of peace," committed to nonviolent resistance of evil and confident in the power of truth, justice, and love. Thus he fought peacefully and boldly against unjust structures while attacking evil at its roots. One might say that his Godbearing life represented faithfully as well as contextually the meaning and the implications of the words in Scripture (adapted from Ps. 85:10–11):

> *Love and Fidelity now meet,*
> *and Justice and Peace now embrace;*
> *Fidelity reaches up from earth*
> *and Justice leans down from heaven.*

Dom Hélder's pacifism was spiritually grounded and nurtured. Together with the study of Scripture and the Catholic social teachings, Gandhi and Martin Luther King, Jr., inspired and modeled for him the way of nonviolent justice-seeking and peacemaking. He became the leading proponent of a nonviolent struggle for liberation in Latin America. Thus he taught and preached on the dignity of the human person and the role of humanity as co-creators with God of the world and its human structures. His consuming passion was the full humanization of people in body, soul, and spirit.

Early on, Dom Hélder realized that unjust structures are present not only in the larger society but also within the church itself. Further, he realized that the church often fails to respond creatively to people's longings for liberation, justice, and peace. He confronted that challenge specifically by leading projects aimed at empowering people to improve their lives and to build a better society. Two of those projects are especially significant in light of the content of this chapter: first, the Movement for Grassroots Education, established in 1961 in collaboration with the Brazilian government; and the movement Action, Justice, and

Peace, founded in 1968 with the backing of Brazilian and other Latin American bishops. The latter initiative was launched on October 2—the 100th anniversary of Gandhi's birthday—with the broad goal of the humanization of Latin American people through economic, political, and social structural change. The movement committed itself explicitly to nonviolence, viewed as positive action and courageous nonconformity with unjust structures.

Education for transformation became a key dimension of these two and other related endeavors. Dom Hélder cooperated with Paulo Freire—one of the great pedagogues and philosophers of education of the twentieth century—in designing educational programs focused on *conscientization,* a neologism coined by Dom Hélder and then widely used. In a nutshell, conscientization is a process of cultural action in which men and women are awakened to their sociocultural reality, move beyond the constraints and alienations to which they are subjected, and affirm themselves as responsible subjects and co-creators of their historical future. With a deepening awareness of the reality that shapes their lives, people can realize their potential and their capacity to transform their society and themselves.[1] Dom Hélder thus highlights the significance of education for personal and social transformation, including the conscientization of oppressors and other privileged people.

> *Anything that is accomplished without educative work,*
> *without preparing minds to accept it, does not take root.*
> *A transformation misunderstood by those who are forced to make concessions*
> *will bring nothing but bitterness and resentment....*
> *It is a dream hard to realize but I hope realizable,*
> *my dream of creative revolutions*
> *that will bring about radical and effective change.*[2]

The remainder of this chapter will consist of an interpretive report on an ongoing project aimed at transformation toward racial justice and reconciliation in the Christian faith community of which I am a member and an ordained minister, the Mennonite Church, USA. It is included in this book honoring Dom Hélder Câmara's life and ministry as a modest illustration of the kind of practical theological task that he graciously inspired and enthusiastically supported.

---

[1] For a systematic presentation and analysis, see Daniel S. Schipani, *Conscientization and Creativity: Paulo Freire and Christian Education* (Lanham: Univ. Pr. of America, 1984); and *Religious Education Encounters Liberation Theology* (Birmingham, Ala.: Religious Education Pr., 1988), chap. 1.

[2] José de Broucker, *Dom Hélder Câmara: The Violence of a Peacemaker,* trans. Herma Briffault (Maryknoll: Orbis Bks., 1970), 56.

The work for dismantling racism, including reflection on this endeavor, may be viewed as a liberation and peace and justice concern within the Mennonite Church. That work is being done primarily through the Damascus Road Project,[3] and it presents a unique challenge to our "historic peace church." The adopted definition of racism is as follows: racial prejudice plus the misuse of systemic and institutional power; further, and simply put, "power" is viewed as (1) racism's power to oppress people of color; (2) racism's ability to give white people power and privilege; and (3) the deeper shaping of people's identity as a direct consequence of racism.

The institution I represent, Associated Mennonite Biblical Seminary (AMBS), became involved in the project in 1999. The seminary is expected to make a unique contribution in light of our theological school's twofold mission—educating Christian leaders and providing theological leadership for the church's teaching ministry.

As anticipated in AMBS's design for participation in the project, my qualitative research focused on the work of several successful Damascus Road teams and programs which have been active since 1996.[4] As part of the research process, I encountered wonderful stories of racial vulnerability, transformation, and ministerial possibilities. In my written and oral communication with the leaders of those Damascus Road teams, I focused on two key, interrelated sets of questions, as follows:

1. What are the fruits of the antiracism endeavors led by Damascus Road teams? What have been the most effective approaches and activities that have contributed (or are contributing) to transforming people's perceptions, attitudes, relationships, and action? What about the experience of educating for transformation (that is, towards racial/social justice and reconciliation)?

---

[3] The Damascus Road Project is an antiracism program started in 1995, designed especially for the historic peace churches in the Anabaptist tradition. Its purpose statement reads: "to lay the groundwork for the long-term work of dismantling racism in Mennonite and Brethren in Christ congregations, conferences, and institutions by training teams from those organizations." To date roughly 500 people from congregations, colleges, church conferences, and church organizations have taken part in antiracism training and started teams working for long-term change. About seventy Mennonite and Brethren in Christ institutions now have Damascus Road teams.

[4] The selection of especially active Damascus Road teams to be studied was done in consultation with the national and regional coordinators. In addition to considering documentation available, direct contact was established with Damascus Road team leaders from Goshen College, Mennonite Board of Congregational Ministries, Fairhaven Mennonite Church (Ft. Wayne, Ind.), Calvary Christian Fellowship (Inglewood, Calif.), and Franconia (Penn.) Conference.

2. How have the understandings and normative convictions concerning peace and justice been confirmed, challenged, expanded, or corrected because of involvement in the Damascus Road process? Has the view of the reign of God been illumined, enhanced, or modified because of the work to dismantle racism? Considering our *Confession of Faith in a Mennonite Perspective*— especially articles 22, 23, 24[5]—in connection with the previous questions, is the content of those articles and commentaries satisfactory as stated? If not, what should be added or changed in order to deepen our understandings and clarify our stated faith convictions?

In the next two sections I summarize several findings pertaining to the questions of identifying transformative practices and significant learnings to be underscored. In the third section I highlight a number of key theological issues and concerns that stem from the Damascus Road project and process. Finally, I indicate four implications of my ongoing research for practical theology and theological education.

TRANSFORMATIVE PRACTICES

Leadership and education

The first observation I have been able to document is that, in all cases studied, effective leadership and focused, deliberate, and intensive educational endeavors play an essential role in effective work of dismantling racism.

Some of the *leadership* issues and factors we were able to identify together are indicated below. The list is not exhaustive but rather illustrative of significant action taken in successful antiracism endeavors:

*   Congregational and other leaders (such as board members and staff persons, administrators, etc.) participated in intensive antiracism training programs.
*   Leaders were able to develop organizing and training competencies in addition to articulating vision and providing overall direction.
*   Antiracism was explicitly included as a specific dimension of leaders' portfolios.
*   There was a deliberate action taken to significantly include "minorities" in leadership committees and actual leadership

---

[5] Articles 22, 23, and 24, respectively, focus on peace, justice, and nonresistance; the church's relationship to government and society; and the reign of God. *Confession of Faith in a Mennonite Perspective* (Scottdale, Pa.: Herald Pr., 1995), 81–92.

positions; for instance, in several cases the intentional increase of "people of color" would reach no less than 20–25 percent of the "full-time equivalent" of a given institution.

- Specific attempts were made to nurture and model interracial and intercultural relationships among the leadership.
- Structures of support were established, such as "racial reconciliation prayer teams," personal intercessors, and others, and accountability for team members as well as some form of auditing for institutions.
- Members of Damascus Road teams were strategically utilized as consultants to congregational and organization leaders.
- Allies and other resources beyond congregations, conferences, and churches were identified and utilized.

Among the *education* issues that we were able to identify as crucial for the success of the efforts to dismantle racism and work toward justice and reconciliation, the following may be highlighted:

- the effectiveness of holding well organized and resourced, intensive workshops for in-depth analysis of racism and power issues, including the importance of developing a shared language and perspective;
- follow up events with a praxis approach aimed at institutional and personal transformation dealing with issues such as structural racism, white privilege, and internalized racist superiority;
- equipping youth and adults to read and study the Bible with an antiracist awareness and commitment to peace with justice;
- teaching and learning the biblical and theological foundations of antiracism as a peace and justice concern;
- equipping youth and adults for direct, nonviolent antiracist action as an appropriate response to divers manifestations of racism;
- educating consistently for peace and justice through preaching and through reflection and action groups;
- teaching and practicing spiritual disciplines—prayer, hospitality, confession and forgiveness, and others—for dismantling racism and working towards transformation and reconciliation;
- promotion of literature and other resources for children, youth, and adults about racism and ways to build genuine multicultural communities.

Ecclesial practices

A second general observation is that congregational transformation becomes apparent in the three essential dimensions of the church's life and ministry, namely, worship, community, and mission.[6] Further, it has been established that intentional antiracism work must take place deliberately within those essential dimensions of the church's life and ministry. Thus, a set of interrelated faith practices necessary for racial justice, as well as the result of the struggle against racism, can be highlighted as follows:

- especially connected with the practices of *worship*: music and singing (which is a discipline and a sacrament for most Mennonites) intentionally becoming more inclusive in worship (leadership, participation, styles, content, language issues, etc.); development of focused, disciplined prayer; revisioning stewardship of money and other dimensions;
- especially connected with the practices of faith *community* life: explicit acknowledgement of brokenness in the body of Christ; confession and testimony in the face of experiences of marginality, exclusion, and inclusion; review and reframing of hospitality; communal discernment for decision-making and action; language awareness and "language care" within congregations and institutions;
- especially connected with the practices of Christian vocation and *mission*: intentional hospitaliy to strangers (minorities particularly); accountability to people of color effectively sought and exercised; prophetic witness (for example, resisting harassment and vandalism perpetrated against members of other ethnic and religious groups and institutions); service to wider community (for instance, providing antiracism training for city council and department heads); people joining the local chapter of the National Association for the Advancement of Colored People; financial support for minority students and others.

LEARNINGS UNDERSCORED

Again, the following list is illustrative of empirically documented outcomes which we have identified as significant as well as potentially transformative:

- For people of color—especially African-American—analysis of racism leads to a heightened awareness of internalized oppression

---

[6] A similar finding is documented in my earlier study of the Reba Place congregation, presented in Daniel S. Schipani, "Education for Social Transformation," in Jack L. Seymour, ed., *Mapping Christian Education: Approaches to Congregational Learning* (Louisville: Abingdon Pr., 1997), 23–40, 130–2.

reflected in low self-esteem and hopelessness (the so-called "sins of the weak") as a starting point for dismantling racism.

- For white people, understandings of white privilege and internalized superiority (so-called "sins of the powerful") are crucial within a "perspective transformation" experience that many describe as nothing short of life-changing, real conversion.[7] In short, transformation is experienced and perceived as new ways of seeing and knowing (vision), of being, valuing and relating (virtue), and of living, working, playing, serving (vocation).
- Youth can play a significant role in the process of unveiling and dismantling racism.
- Opportunities may be created and made available for reading the Bible differently, namely, welcoming diverse perspectives.
- Potential exists for deepening ethical and theological reflection (e.g., around foci such as sinfulness and evil, violence and nonviolence, divine-human partnerships, possibilities of transformation, reconciliation and healing, and so on).
- Consistent work to dismantle racism helps the church and church-related institutions to reclaim some lost credibility with people of color over historical issues of racism, slavery, and many others.

REVISITING PEACE THEOLOGY

Participants in the Damascus Road Project sooner or later encounter key theological issues and questions. Unfortunately, however, we have not found evidence of significant and intentional biblical-theological reflection involving issues and questions such as the following (which were identified in conversation with my interviewees):

- Peace and justice are found to be, indeed, central to the gospel: a normative conviction that is commonly reconfirmed and directly related not only to the moral and political teachings of Jesus but to the soteriological questions of the atonement as well.[8]

---

[7] Indeed, successful antiracism work provides, among other things, a clear illustration of the kind of transformative learnings and growth associated with concepts such as "conscientization" and "paradigm/perspective transformation" in the fields of critical pedagogy and adult learning research and theory.

[8] On this and related theological issues, see Gayle Gerber Koontz's essay, "The Liberation of Atonement," *MQR* 63 (April 1989): 171–92. See also Daniel S. Schipani, ed. *Freedom and Discipleship: Liberation Theology in an Anabaptist Perspective* (Maryknoll: Orbis Bks., 1989); in the final article of that book, "Implications for Peace and Justice Witness," Leroy Friesen helpfully summarizes fundamental questions that must be raised, such as, "What are the biblical teachings as to the nature and extent of the lordship of the Risen Christ, and what view of the world is rooted in the degree of expansiveness of that lordship? ...Is invitation

- Peace theology as such may and should be enhanced with the explicit and concrete inclusion of justice, due to the reality of racism and the struggle to dismantle it; hence, a more comprehensive "shalom theology" may be embraced together with the perceived tension involving "discipleship" and "citizenship."[9]
- By the same token, participants in antiracism endeavors discover that a (passive) nonresistance stance—a significant strain for Mennonites as a historic peace church—needs to be challenged and corrected. The language of nonresistance appears too restrictive, protective of the church as such,[10] as if the church were primarily focused on maintaining its own purity while avoiding direct involvement in the public arena. In sum, this perspective and commitment illustrate the revolutionary ethical and theological movement from *pacifism as nonresistance* (essentially, for the church only) to *peacemaking as nonviolent resistance* to evil for the sake of social justice in light of the reign of God.
- Nonviolent resistance is considered an appropriate response to racism; it is also viewed as a special case of ministry in solidarity with oppressed and victimized people.[11] More specifically, the

---

to justice-making in the larger society part of the Good News of shalom? (justicemaking understood in the biblical sense of God's call to the righting of relationships)" (177).

[9] John A. Coleman makes a helpful contribution in this regard, in "The Two Pedagogies: Discipleship and Citizenship," in Mary C. Boys, ed., *Education for Citizenship and Discipleship* (New York: Pilgrim, 1989), chap. 2. Coleman—who discusses John Howard Yoder and Jon Sobrino, among others—insightfully argues that the church must educate for both discipleship and citizenship, and that they must be integrated. He demonstrates that, on the one hand, discipleship may add to citizenship the values and alternatives of utopia, counterculture, and vocation; on the other hand, citizenship may add certain qualities to discipleship: (a) it widens the reach of Christian solidarity by reminding the church that God's grace reigns outside its contours and that the community of faith exists for the world; (b) in the often intractable day-to-day reality of politics, it teaches humility so that Christian citizens learn the way of shared responsibility and solidarity in history; and (c) it represents a reality test, an experiential proving ground for Christian claims for this-worldly, liberative, restorative potential in grace and redemption so that Christians put flesh on their hopes for a transformed future, the new creation based on the transforming power of Christ in history.

[10] A classic work focusing on the nonresistance motif as the guiding principle of an Anabaptist peace theology is Guy F. Hershberger, *War, Peace, and Nonresistance* (Scottdale: Herald Pr., 1944). Consideration of several other current peace theology streams—including "radical pacifism," "social responsibility," "political pacifism," and "liberation pacifism"—can be found in John Richard Burkholder and Barbara Nelson Gingerich, eds. *Mennonite Peace Theology: A Panorama of Types* (Akron: Mennonite Central Committee Peace Office, 1991).

[11] For a thorough study that traces significant changes in the practices and normative convictions of Mennonites in the twentieth century, see Leo Driedger and Donald B.

struggle for racial justice and reconciliation reveals that siding with the oppressed and marginalized people is a requirement, even if taking sides is not done in narrow partisan ways. It is impossible to be neutral. In other words, a kind of "preferential option" on behalf of the victims of racial injustice is a necessary dimension of the efforts to dismantle racism. For many Mennonites, however, nonviolent confrontation is controversial, particularly with regard to practices of advocacy, strategizing, organizing, and acting in the midst of social and political conflict at institutional, personal, and structural levels.

- The relationship between "peace and justice" and "mission evangelism" needs to be reenvisioned in light of new questions and challenges (for example, how to relate to people of color who happen to be non-Christian).

- The view of God's reign[12] needs to be illuminated and enhanced in connection with the work to dismantle racism. For instance, a more holistic and comprehensive view of salvation is required (that is, more than individual and personal; historical as well as eschatological; involving people outside the church, etc.). Also needed are new images and perspectives to visualize, long for, and participate in the "normative culture" of the reign of God.

Kraybill, *Mennonite Peacemaking: From Quietism to Activism* (Scottdale: Herald Pr., 1994). Sociologists Dridger and Kraybill document the influences shaping the emergence of active peacemaking between 1950 and 1990 within four categories of macro forces: societal (urbanization, education, mobility, individuation); political (civil rights, Vietnam war, nuclear arms, women's rights, Central America); denominational (missionary experience, MCC service overseas, I-W and voluntary service in the USA); and theological (recovery of an "Anabaptist vision," ecumenical conversations and collaboration, liberation theology). The outcomes identified include a number of institutional programs, such as Christian Peacemaker Teams, Victim Offender Reconciliation Program, Mennonite Conciliation Services, local peace centers, criminal justice ministries, Women's Concerns, etc., in addition to the production of literature and other resources, such as curriculum materials. Ongoing antiracism work obviously continues and enhances this development in which justice becomes an essential part of the shalom theology of an increasingly public church.

[12] Article 24 of *Confession of Faith in a Mennonite Perspective*, "The Reign of God," is found to be woefully inadequate in that it reduces the vision to our hope beyond history. It is only in the explication of the article that we find a reference to the church being called "to live now according to the model of the future reign of God;" and in the commentary section we read that "the reign of God is relevant to this world, and the ethics of God's rule [as embodied in our life together] should not be postponed to some future time." However, there is no reference whatsoever to the possibility of discerning the reigning of God beyond the "life together" of the church, let alone the possibility of being called to participate in liberating and reconciling work—where God is supposedly at work as well—beyond the contours of the mission of the ecclesial community narrowly defined.

IMPLICATIONS FOR PRACTICAL THEOLOGY AND THEOLOGICAL EDUCATION

Finally, I wish to highlight four sets of observations which stem from my research and which merit further discussion and reflection, as indicated in the following paragraphs.

First, the study suggests that it is possible to detect fundamental analogies and structural continuities among the following interrelated areas: (a) faith-based and ministry practices aimed at dismantling racism; (b) corresponding theoretical reflection (as, for instance in my own theory of education for peace and justice);[13] (c) pertinent curriculum and pedagogy questions of theological education (what to teach, and how best to teach for peace and justice in our theological schools); and (d) constructing practical theology.[14]

Second, the study confirms the essential place and role of practical theology as a theological discipline understood as a theory of action. In Gerben Heitink's helpful conceptualization, such a theory of action involves hermeneutical (understanding), empirical (explanation), and strategic (action/change) dimensions.[15] Actually, focusing on the challenge of racism in the USA provides an opportunity for further exploration regarding the following: (a) commonalities among diverse conceptualizations of practical theology as a theological theory of action; and (b) the contribution of practical theology to a theory of ecclesial, social, and personal transformation.

Third, the study further points to the possible complementarity among different settings and levels of theologizing, and educating and working for peace and justice, such as congregations, theological schools,

---

[13] Daniel S. Schipani, *Religious Education Encounters Liberation Theology;* "Liberation Theology and Religious Education," in *Theologies of Religious Education,* ed. Randolph Crump Miller (Birmingham, Ala.: Religious Education Pr., 1995), 286–313; "Education for Social Transformation"; and Daniel S. Schipani and Paulo Freire, *Educación, Libertad y Creatividad: Encuentro y Diálogo con Paulo Freire,* 2nd. ed. (San Juan: Universidad Interamericana de Puerto Rico, 1998).

[14] A number of studies have considered the relationship between practical theology and Christian religious education; see for instance, Don Browning, "Religious Education As Growth in Practical Theological Reflection and Action," in *Education for Citizenship and Discipleship,* ed. Mary C. Boys, 133–62; Richard R. Osmer, "Teaching As Practical Theology," in *Theological Approaches to Christian Education,* ed. Jack L. Seymour and Donald E. Miller, (Nashville: Abingdon Pr., 1990), 216–38, 283–7. Also, Robert O'Gorman has recently suggested that a practical theological approach such as Browning's offers us a way to analyze theological pedagogy from a practical theology perspective (in APT's Occasional Papers no. 4 (spring 2000): 2–5). I am not aware, however, of any study that explores main fundamental analogies and structural continuities as suggested above.

[15] See Gerber Heitink, *Practical Theology: History. Theory. Action Domains,* trans. Reinder Bruinsma (Grand Rapids: Eerdmans, 1999).

and other church-based institutions.[16] Our research also underscores (a) the challenge to find a common language and methodology to make communication and collaboration possible;[17] (b) potential mutual enrichment and partnership; and (c) the need for mutual accountability in addition to the requisite of accountability to people of color.

Fourth and finally, the research calls for the explicit inclusion of two essential features in theological and educational endeavors. Those features are (a) (paradoxical) clarity in regard to the theological vision which undergirds and orients our praxis, that is, wisdom in the light of God together with a commitment to participate in God's trinitarian praxis in the world and for the sake of the world; and (b) a communal and personal spirituality as an essential dimension of all the processes involved,[18] in the actual ministry for racial justice and reconciliation, in theological education, and in doing practical theology.

At the end of this discussion, we are again reminded of the extraordinary example of Dom Hélder's life and ministry. Like him, we are called to integrate the outward ministry of justice, peacemaking, and reconciliation with the inner journey of contemplation, meditation, and reflection. Service and prayer must embrace each other so our call may be fulfilled, for in the last analysis our human vocation is to become partners with the creative, liberating, healing, and empowering Spirit of God. As Dom Hélder used to pray:

---

[16] Thus, borrowing imagery from Latin American liberation theologians, we might say that a tree of praxis as well as a tree of theology may be visualized as follows: first, we have the level of congregational or grassroots peace and justice witness and theologizing; second, the trunk of such a tree is represented, for example, by Mennonite institutions and programs such as Damascus Road antiracism project and certain peace statements (especially helpful is the 1993 statement of Mennonite Central Committee, "A Commitment to Christ's Way of Peace"); and third, the limbs and foliage of the tree are represented by academic involvement and reflection, such as the substantial contributions of AMBS faculty in our systematic work on the Bible, history, theology and ethics, and practical theology pertaining to peace and justice concerns.

[17] For instance, I find that one way to encourage ethical-theological reflection on the congregational level, as well as conversation and collaboration across levels of theologizing is by consistently raising fundamental practical questions such as, "How shall we love the neighbors who are oppressed and victimized by racism?"

[18] James W. Fowler alludes to the questions of theological vision and spirituality I wish to underscore, in the context of his discussion of common characteristics of practical theological approaches, in "The Emerging New Shape of Practical Theology: New Life for Practical Theology," in *Pastoral-Theologische Informationen* 16, no. 2 (December 1996): 205–23; see especially the references to practical theology reclaiming the approaches of a theology habitus, practical theology working in two languages—the "language behind the wall" and the "language on the wall"—and the need for shared visions of the praxis of God and of human vocation.

Don't extinguish the light of your presence within me.
O Lord, look through my eyes,
listen through my ears,
speak through my lips,
walk with my feet.
Lord, may my poor human presence
be a reminder, however weak,
of your divine presence.[19]

---

[19] Quoted from a prayer of Cardinal Newman, in "A Most Transparent Life: Interview with Dom Hélder Câmara," *Sojourners* 16, no. 11 (December 1987), 17.

"It is clear that, loving everyone, I must have special love, like Christ, for the poor."

Appendix
Providence has taken me by the hand

DOM HÉLDER CÂMARA

Providence has taken me by the hand
and led me to Olinda and Recife;
Pope Paul VI, who has a deep knowledge
of Latin America and Brazil,
decided that this key position of North-East Brazil
should be filled without delay.

It is a divine grace
to be able to detect the signs of the times,
to be abreast of modern developments,
to participate fully in the plan of God.
Let us examine together what is taking place....

Who am I, and to whom am I speaking or trying to speak?
I am a native of the North-East
addressing other natives of the North-East,
with eyes turned to Brazil,
to Latin America,
and to the world.
A human creature who regards himself

In April 1964, Paul VI designated as archbishop of Olinda and Recife Dom Hélder Câmara, then bishop auxiliary to the cardinal of Rio de Janeiro and secretary of the Brazilian Episcopal Conference. On the occasion of his installation as archbishop on April 12 of that year, Dom Hélder addressed this message to the people of his archdiocese. The text has been edited for inclusion here.

as brother in weakness and in sin to all human beings
of all races and all religions of the world.
I am a Christian
who addresses himself to Christians,
but with heart open, ecumenically,
to people of every creed and ideology.
A bishop of the Catholic church who comes,
in the imitation of Christ,
not to be served but to serve.

Catholics and non-Catholics,
believers and nonbelievers,
all of you accept my brotherly greetings:
"May Jesus Christ be praised!"

The bishop belongs to all
Let no one be scandalized
if I frequent those who are considered unworthy and sinful.
Who is not a sinner?
Who can throw the first stone?
Our Lord,
charged with visiting publicans and eating with sinners,
replied that it is the sick who have need of the doctor.

Let no one be alarmed
if I am seen with compromising and dangerous people,
of the left or the right,
of establishment or opposition,
with reformist or anti-reformist,
revolutionary or anti-revolutionary,
with those of good faith or bad.
Let no one claim to bind me to a group,

so that I should consider that person's friends to be mine
and make my own that person's hostilities.
My door and my heart will be open to everyone,
absolutely everyone.
Christ died for all;
I must exclude no one from dialogue.

Concern for the poor

It is clear that, loving everyone,
I must have special love,
like Christ,
for the poor.
At the last judgment,
we shall all be judged by our treatment of Christ,
of Christ who hungers and thirsts,
who is dirty, injured, and oppressed.

Continuing the existing work of our archdiocese,
I shall care for the poor,
being particularly concerned that poverty
should not degenerate into misery.
Poverty can and at times must be accepted generously
or offered spontaneously as a gift to the Father.
But misery is degrading and repellent;
it destroys the image of God that is in each of us;
it violates the right and duty of human beings
to strive for personal fulfillment.

It is obvious that I am thinking in a special way
of the people in the slums and the abandoned children.
Whoever is suffering in body or in spirit,
whether rich or poor,

whoever is desperate,
shall have a special place in the heart of the bishop.

But I do not wish to deceive anyone,
as though a little generosity and social assistance
were sufficient.
Without a doubt there are spectacular miseries
that give us no right to remain indifferent.
Often the only thing to do is to give immediate help.
However, let us not think that the problem
is limited to certain slight reforms
and let us not confuse
the good and indispensable notion of order,
the goal of all human progress,
with caricatures of it
that are responsible for the persistence of structures
that everyone recognizes cannot be preserved.

If we wish to tackle the roots of our social evils,
we must help our country to break the vicious circle
of underdevelopment and misery.
Some people are scandalized
that this should be our primary problem.
Others question the sincerity of our motives....

It would be scandalous and unforgivable
if the church were to abandon the masses
in their hour of greatest need;
they would think we had no interest in helping them
to achieve a degree of human and Christian dignity
and to raise themselves to the category of people.

Human values to be developed

We are all convinced
that all human beings
are children of the same heavenly Father.
Those who have the same father are brothers and sisters;
let us treat one another as brothers and sisters.

We are all convinced
that God made human beings
in God's own image and likeness
and entrusted to them the mission
of caring for nature and completing the work of creation.
Let us do everything possible
or impossible
that work in the North-East
may be truly a participation
in the work of our Creator.

We are all convinced
that freedom is a divine gift
that must be preserved at any price.
Let us liberate,
in the fullest sense of the word,
every human creature in our midst.

We are all convinced
that our ideal
is the development of each and every creature among us.

There are not lacking today
examples of religious indifference and atheism
among highly-developed nations.

Our own development project does not seek to exclude God.
The more we progress materially,
the greater will be our need of a strong, clear faith
capable of illuminating from within
the construction of the new North-East....

The church has no wish to dominate the course of events.
The church is here to serve human beings,
to help them be free.
And the church will be ready to affirm
that this process of liberation,
that begins in time,
cannot be fully accomplished until the end of time,
the true beginning when the Son of God returns.

You will have noticed
that the North-East is at once
a national problem
and a center of international attention.

But the image that is presented of us,
both at home and abroad,
is invariably false.

The world looks to the North-East
By now the North-East is a cliché,
a slogan.
The North-East does not accept this standardization of misery,
and cannot, must not,
accept classification as the most explosive area
of Latin America.

Let us be united in making the North-East
an anticipation of tomorrow's Brazil,
of the future Latin America,
and of the new face of the Third World.
Let us be united
because no authentic development
can be restricted to one group or to one class.
Either the entire region is developed,
with all its human groupings,
or development is distorted.

It is for this reason that I do not just appeal
to management and workers,
to rich and poor,
to left and right,
to believer and nonbeliever,
that they should agree on a truce.
It is essential to begin,
trustingly,
a crescendo of dialogue.
It would be a grave matter
before the judgment of God and of history
to withdraw ourselves
from the reconstruction of the world.

As part of Brazil and Latin America,
we bear the responsibility of being the Christian portion,
the Christian continent,
of the Third World.
Clearly we do not claim to be superior or better
than our Asian and African brothers and sisters.
But we have greater responsibility....

Christ is José, Antonio, Severino

Let us press on without delay with the task of development
as a Christian means of evangelizing.
What value can there be in venerating pretty images of Christ,
or even recognizing his disfigured face in that of the poor,
if we fail to identify him with human beings
who need to be rescued from their underdeveloped condition.

However strange it may seem to some,
Christ in the North-East is called
José,
Antonio,
Severino...
Behold the man!
This is Christ,
the person who needs justice,
who has a right to justice,
who deserves justice.
If we are to avoid sterile and destructive violence
on the part of the oppressed,
we must look beyond the appearance of harmony
that makes dialogue impossible....

Everyone knows and shouts about the need
for radical reform in our country.
In the past there has been mistrust of the reformers
and the constant fear of communist infiltration.
Now that the situation has changed there is no time to lose.
The desired reforms must come without delay.
Let them be just and balanced,
but on no account must they give
the impression of mystification.

The reforms should come in a spontaneous way and,
above all,
without rancor or ill-feeling.
Let the Brazilian people be incapable of hatred,
realizing that this is the greatest sin,
since God is charity,
God is love.

As for the North-East,
which begins its development
against a background of depressions and hopes,
let it be an example to the whole country
of a dynamic peace founded on justice,
of truth rooted in charity,
of dialogue and understanding that transcend divisions
capable of dragging the country into civil war and chaos.

Let the North-East be an example to the whole of Brazil
of a speedy recovery from political crisis.
Without prejudice to national security measures
of vigilance towards communism,
let us not accuse of communism
those who simply hunger and thirst for social justice
and the development of our country.
Let us help Brazil not to destroy the hopes of the people.

We shall prove that democracy is capable of tackling
the very roots of our social evil....

Instead of trying to reform others,
let us first reform ourselves.
The difference between the pharisees and the saints

is that the pharisees are big-hearted with themselves
and strict with others,
trying to force them into heaven.
Saints are rigorous only with themselves;
with sinners they are as generous as the goodness of God,
boundless as the mercy of the Father....

The time of ecumenism
Being moved still by the spirit of the Council,
we encourage all our people to keep in mind at all times
—in our meetings, in our studies, in our prayer—
not only those of other religions,
but also those who are unaffiliated to any church.
I have a particular regard for people of no faith,
who wander in darkness,
especially when they are atheist in name but Christian in deed.

To those who constitute "the world," as we call it,
I repeat the inspired words of Paul VI:
"Let the world know that the church looks on it
with profound understanding,
with sincere admiration,
and with the genuine intention not of conquering it,
but of serving it;
not of despising it,
but of appreciating it;
not of condemning it,
but of strengthening and saving it."

The devout who hear my words
are probably thinking that their bishop
is more concerned with the strayed sheep

than with the ninety-nine who never abandoned the flock.
But isn't this precisely the attitude
of the Good Shepherd?

Obviously we shall have time also
for our revered and devoted faithful.
Our work with them will be inspired
by the transfiguration of the Lord,
the title of our archdiocese:
by our baptism we are made one with Christ.
Instead of a worn and faded Christ,
it is necessary that he be transfigured in us
as he was on Mount Tabor.
Our Lady,
patroness of Olinda and Recife,
will assist in the glorification of her Son
in and through us.

Do you remember the moving spectacle
at the death of Pope John XXIII?
This unforgettable scene is,
I am sure,
lesson for all of us.
Catholics and non-Catholics,
believers and nonbelievers,
people of all races, creeds, and ideologies
suffered with the pope in his last agony
and lamented his death
as the death of a father,
thereby manifesting the implicit desire of the people:
a prelate,
a bishop must be good like Pope John.

Pray to your heavenly Father,
the giver of every grace and every light,
that this may be the livery of your new bishop;
that he may remind you of Pope John XXIII.
This will be an excellent way of reminding you
of Christ himself,
the Good Shepherd.

A selected bibliography of the works of Dom Hélder Câmara

A Universidade e a Integracão National. Campina Grande: Fundacão Universidade Regional do Nordeste, [1968].

Brazil. LADOC "Keyhole" series, 8. Washington: Division for Latin America, USCC, [1974].

Christianismo, socialismo, capitalismo. Translated by Angel García Fluixá and Alfonso Ortiz. Salamanca: Ediciones Sígueme, 1979.

The Church and Colonialism. Translated by William McSweeney. London: Sheed and Ward, 1969.

Complicità o resistenza?: La Chiesa in America Latina: Interviste a H. Câmara, M. Silva, A. B. Fragoso, Frei Betto, G. Lebret, J. S. Solar, P. Freire. Interviewed by Linda Bimbi. Assisi: Citadella editrice, 1976.

Croire, c'est simple: paroles de vie. Mesnil Saint-Loup: Le Livre ouvert, 1988.

The Desert Is Fertile. Translated by Dinah Livingstone. Maryknoll: Orbis Bks., 1981.

Dom Hélder Câmara, the Conversions of a Bishop: An Interview with José de Broucker. Translated by Hilary Davies. London: Collins, 1979.

Dom Hélder Câmara vous parle: le combat mondial pour la justice et la paix; message de dom Hélder Câmara et réponses aux questions. Lyon, France: Palais des Sports, 1970.

Dom Hélder discursos internacionais. Recife: Arquidiocese de Olinda e Recife, 1980.

Dom Hélder: 80 anos de amor à vida. Dom do amor. Recife: Obras de Frei Francisco, 1989.

El grito del Tercer Mundo en un pueblo marginado: ¿Milagro brasileño?: testimonios Hélder Câmara y otros obispos de Brasil. Buenos Aires: Merayo Editor, 1974.

El Manifesto de los obispos del tercer mundo: una respuesta al clamor de los pobres. Comentarios de Alberto Devota [y] Hélder Câmara. [Avellaneda]: Ediciones Búsqueda, 1968.

Escritos sobre la teología de la liberación en Latínoamérica, by Mario Bendetti. [Buenos Aires]: Instituto de Estudios Latinoamericanos, [1984].

Família: missão de amor. São Paulo: Paulinas, 1997.

Hélder Câmara. LADOC "Keyhole" series, 12. Washington: Latin America Documentation, 1975.

Hélder Câmara; escritos. Prologue and notes by Paulo Schilling. Buenos Aires: Schapire, 1972.

Hélder Câmara: Works 1976–1985. Recife: Arquidiocese de Olinda e Recife, 1976–1985. Text-fiche.

Hélder Câmara y la justicia: ideario. Edited by Benedicto Tapia de Renedo. Salamanca: Ediciones Sígueme, 1981.

Hoping against All Hope. Translated by Matthew J. O'Connell. Maryknoll: Orbis Bks., 1984.

Ideario de Hélder Câmara, 2d ed. Edited by Feliciano Blázquez. Salamanca, Spain: Ediciones Sígueme, 1981.

"If You Want Peace, Work towards Justice." Kansas City, Kans.: Economic Conference on the Vietnam War, 1972.

Into Your Hands, Lord. Translated by Alan Neame. London: Darton, Longman and Todd, 1987.

Introduction to *O drama do evangelho: na liturgia, na pastoral, no teatro.* By Isaac Gondim Filho. Petrópolis: Vozes, 1982.

It's Midnight, Lord. Translated by Joseph Gallagher with Thomas Fuller and Tom Conry; illustrated by Naul Ojeda. Washington: The Pastoral Pr., 1984.

J'ai entendu les cris de mon peuple. Paris: La Procure, [1975].

Juventude e dominação cultural. Edited by Ismar de Oliveira Soares, Reinaldo Matias Fleuri. São Paulo: Edições Paulinas, 1982.

La Iglesia debe revisar su posición ante los problemas sociales. [Paraâiba: [s.n.], 1966].

La Iglesia en el desarrollo de América Latina. 2d ed. Madrid: Zero, 1970.

La rebelión de los economistas. 3d ed. Bilbao: Zero, 1973.

La universidad y el desarrollo de América Latina; conferencia pronunciada por d. Hélder Câmara, Arzobispo de Olinda y Recife, en ocasión de la apertura del año académico en la Universidad Católica de Chile, Santiago, 19 de abril de 1969. [Santiago de Chile, 1969].

Lateinamerika: Beitr. / von Dom Hélder Câmara...[et al.]. Friedenbulletin; 4. Stuttgart: Grohmann, [1975].

Le rosaire de dom Hélder. Translated by Fatima Braz Panthier; introduction by Fatima Braz Panthier et José de Broucker; postscript by Gilles Baudery. Paris: Desclée de Brouwer, 1997.

"Lo que se hace sin formar una mentalidad no tiene sentido; reportaje." In *Evangelio y justicia,* 2nd ed. Algorta: Zero, 1970.

Memória viva de Dom Hélder Câmara. [Brazil]: Nossa Editora, [1989].

Nossa Senhora no Meu Camino: Meditacões do Padre Josâe. São Paulo: Edições Paulinas, 1983.

Palavras e reflexões. Recife: Editora Universitária da UFPF, 1995.

Pobreza, abundancia y solidaridad. 3d ed. Bilbao: Zero, 1973.

Questions for Living. Translated by Robert R. Barr. Maryknoll: Orbis Bks., 1987.

Quién no necesita convertirse? Buenos Aires: Paulinas, 1991.

Quién soy yo?: autocrítica. Madrid: Sociedad de Educación Atenas, 1978.

Race against Time. Translated by Della Couling. London: Sheed and Ward, 1971.

Revolution through Peace. Translated by Amparo McLean. New York: Harper & Row, 1972.

Sister Earth: Creation, Ecology and the Spirit. Foreword by Albert LaChance. Hyde Park: New City Pr., 1995.

Spiral of Violence. London: Sheed and Ward, 1975.

Structures of Injustice. London: Justice and Peace Commission, [1972].

The Third World, a Problem of Justice. [s.l.: s.n.], 1975.

A Thousand Reasons for Living. Philadelphia: Fortress Press, 1981.

Through the Gospel with Dom Hélder Câmara. Translated by Alan Neame. Maryknoll: Orbis Bks., 1986.

Une journée avec don Hélder Câmara. [Bruxelles: Desclée, De Brouwer, 1970].

Universidad y revolución. Textos seleccionados por Fernando Reyes Matta. [Santiago]: Ediciones Nueva Universidad, Universidad Católica de Chile, [1969].

Um olhar sobre a cidade. Rio de Janeiro: Civilização Brasileira, 1979.

Un vent de révolte, où, La verité étouffée. Interviewed by Edith-France Lesprit. [s.l.]: Sangwan Surasarang, 1980.

Utopias peregrinas. [Recife:] Editora Universitária, UFPE, [1993?]

Umsturz durch die Gewaltlosen; eine Initiative. Hélder Câmara antwortet Ulrich Stockmann, by Ulrich Stockmann. Das Theologische Interview, 25. [Düsseldorf]: Patmos, [1971].

"Violent Pacifist Liberationist man of God—Dom Hélder Câmara: Dom Hélder Câmara et la Violence des Pacifiques." *Cooperation Canada* 20 (May/June 1975): 3–9

Selected writings on Dom Hélder Câmara

Bandino, Lino. *Dom Hélder Câmara: Hermano de los pobres.* Santiago: Salesiana, 1982.

Brooke, James. "Two Archbishops, Old and New, Symbolize Conflict in the Brazilian Church." *New York Times* 139 (12 November 1989): 4.

Brown, Robert MacAfee. "Spirituality and Liberation." *St. Luke's Journal of Theology* 29 (June 1986): 3.

Broucker, José de. *Dom Hélder Câmara: The Violence of a Peacemaker.* Translated by Herma Briffault. Maryknoll: Orbis Bks., 1970.

Caramuru Barros, Raimundo, and Lauro de Oliveira. *Dom Hélder: o artesão da paz.* Brasília: Senado Federal, 2000.

Casey-Rutland, Ransom Eugene. "An Examination of the Issue of Violence in the Writings of Selected Latin American Liberation Theologians." Ph.D. diss., Emory University, 1991.

Cavilliotti, Martha. *Hélder Câmara, la crisis en la Iglesia en América Latina* Buenos Aires: Centro Editor de América Latina, 1985.

Cheetham, Neville. *Hélder Câmara.* London: S.C.M. Press, 1973.

Cirano, Marcos. *Os caminhos de Dom Hélder: perseguições e censura, 1964–1980.* Recife: Editora Guararapes, 1983.

Cook, Guillermo. *The Expectation of the Poor: Latin American Basic Ecclesial Communities in Protestant Perspective.* Maryknoll: Orbis Bks., 1985.

Cunneen, Sally. "The Good News from Latin America." *Christian Century* 98 (7–14 January 1981): 5–6.

Eigenmann, Urs. *Hélder Câmara: Prophetischer Bischof.* Freiburg: Kanisius, 1992.

———. *Politische Praxis des Glaubens: Dom Hélder Câmaras Weg zum Anwalt der Armen und seine Reden an die Reichen.* Freiburg: Edition Exodus, Edition Liberacíon, 1984.

Foley, Michael. *Crusaders for the Poor in Latin America: Hélder Câmara and Oscar Romero.* Bangor: Welsh National Centre for Religious Education, 1996.

González-Balado, José Luis. *Me llaman el obispo rojo: Dom Hélder Câmara.* Barcelona: Ediciones Paulinas, 1974.

Hall, Mary. *A Quest for the Liberated Christian: Examination on the Basis of a Mission, a Man and a Movement As Agents of Liberation.* Frankfurt am Main: Lang, 1978.

———. *The Impossible Dream: The Spirituality of Dom Hélder Câmara.* Belfast: Christian Journals Ltd., 1979.

Hornman, Wim. *De rode bisschop: Roman over Dom Hélder Câmara.* Utrecht: Spectrum, 1985.

Kathen, Nelmo Roque Ten. *Uma vida para os pobres:Eespiritualidade de Dom Hélder Câmara.* São Paulo, Brasil: Edições Loyola, 1991.

Kemper, Vicki. "A Worker for God's Church of the Poor." *Sojourners* 16 (December 1987): 4.

———, and Larry Engle. "A Prophet's Vision and Grace: The Life of Dom Hélder Câmara." *Sojourners* 16 (December 1987): 12–15.

Leonard, Patrick Joseph. "Dom Hélder Câmara: A Study in Polarity." Ph.D. diss., St. Louis University, 1974.

Lernoux, Penny. "In Common Suffering and Hope." *Sojourners* 16 (December 1987): 22–5.

Marin, Richard. *Dom Hélder Câmara, les puissants et les pauvres: pour une histoire de l'Eglise des pauvres dans le Nordeste brésilien, 1955–1985.* Paris: Editions de l'atelier/Editions ouvrières, 1995.

Meunier, Paul. *Ils ont changé le monde: Gandhi, Dom Hélder Câmara, Raoul Follereau.* Montréal: Éditions Paulines, 1994.

Moosbrugger, Bernhard, and Gladys Weigner. *A Voice of the Third World: Dom Hélder Câmara.* New York: Paulist Pr., 1972.

Nute, Betty Richardson. *Hélder Câmara's Latin America.* London: Friends Peace and International Relations Committee, 1974.

Oliveira, Harrison. *Dom Hélder: O prisioneiro do Vaticano.* Varzea: Editora Universitaria, 1999.

Piletti, Nelson. *Dom Hélder Câmara: entre o poder e a profecia.* São Paulo: Editora Atica, 1997.

Pomerleau, Claude. "A Day with Dom Hélder." *Sojourners* 5 (July-August 1976) 18–19.

Potrick, Maria Bernarda. *Dom Hélder Câmara: testigo del evangelio en América Latina.* Translated by María Laura Barral de Mallimaci. Buenos Aires: Ediciones Paulinas, 1986.

Rocha, Abelardo Baltar da. *Um furacão varre a esperança: O caso D. Hélder.* Recife: FUNDARPE, 1993.

Rocha, Zildo. *Hélder, o dom: uma vida que marcou os rumos da Igreja no Brasil.* Petrópolis: Editora Vozes, 1999.

Rossi, J. J. and Dom Hélder Câmara. *Iglesia y desarrollo.* 3rd. ed. [Buenos Aires]: Ediciones Busqueda, 1973.

Santa Ana, Julio de. "Through the Third World towards One World." *Exchange* 19 (December 1990): 217–35.

Schmitz, Gerald Joseph. "Revolution through Peace? An Inquiry into the Meaning and Significance of the Thought of Dom Hélder Câmara in the Light of 'Political Theology' and the Quest for a Gospel of Liberation." Ph.D. diss., Carleton University, 1978.

Skudlarek, William. "A Most Transparent Life: Brazil's Pastor of the Poor, An Interview." *Sojourners* 16 (December 1987): 16–20.

Ssemakula, Luke. "How the Spiritual Vision of Pierre Teilhard de Chardin Influenced the Life and Ministry of Dom Hélder Câmara." Thesis, Jesuis School of Theology at Berkeley, 2000.

Suenes, Cardinal Léon-Joseph. *Charismatic Renewal and Social Action: A Dialogue / Cardinal Léon-Joseph Suenes and Dom Hélder Câmara.* Malines document, 3. Ann Arbor: Servant Bks., 1979.

Tapia de Renedo, Benedicto. *Hélder Câmara, signo de contradicción.* Salamanca: Sígueme, 1974.

Toulat, Jean. *Dom Hélder Câmara.* Paris: Centurion, 1989.

Put your ear to the ground
and listen,
hurried, worried footsteps,
bitterness, rebellion.
Hope
hasn't yet begun.
Listen again.
Put out feelers.
The Lord is there.
He is far less likely
to abandon us
in hardship
than in times of ease.

Dom Hélder Câmara
The Desert Is Fertile

Dom Hélder is honored in many ways, including having a street named after him in the city of Delft, the Netherlands.

Dom Hélder Câmara speaks on the occasion of receiving the honorary doctorate in social sciences from the Free University, October 20, 1975.

Dom Hélder speaks at the centennial anniversary of the Free University and calls for the establishment of a chair for justice, liberation, and peace.

To order additional copies of *The Promise of Hope: A Tribute to Dom Hélder,* please contact:

Institute of Mennonite Studies
3003 Benham Avenue
Elkhart IN 46517-1999
574-296-6239
e-mail ims@ambs.edu
www.ambs.edu/IMS